THE BIG BOOK OF BORIS

THE BIG BOOK OF
BORIS

COMPILED BY
IAIN DALE &
JAKUB SZWEDA

Biteback Publishing

First published in Great Britain in 2019 by
Biteback Publishing Ltd
Westminster Tower
3 Albert Embankment
London SE1 7SP
Selection and editorial apparatus copyright © Iain Dale & Jakub Szweda 2019

Iain Dale & Jakub Szweda have asserted their rights under the Copyright,
Designs and Patents Act 1988 to be identified as the editors of this work.

This book is an updated version of *The Little Book of Boris*,
published by Harriman House in 2007.

Illustrations courtesy of Hoby, www.hobycartoons.com

ISBN 978-1-78590-548-3

10 9 8 7 6 5 4 3 2 1

A CIP catalogue record for this book is available from the British Library.

Set in Minion Pro

Printed and bound in Great Britain by
CPI Group (UK) Ltd, Croydon CR0 4YY

CONTENTS

PREFACE

There are few politicians who could genuinely be described as a phenomenon. Boris Johnson is one. Whatever 'it' is, he's got it in spades. Walk down the street with him and he is mobbed by people wanting selfies. Borismania happened way before Corbynmania became a 'thing'.

Boris's appearances on *Have I Got News For You* propelled him into the political stratosphere, building him a fan base way beyond the confines of politics. Boris has star quality. He's loved by many, ridiculed by some and feared by others.

My abiding memory of Boris was spending a day with him when I was campaigning as the Conservative Party candidate in North Norfolk back in 2004. Boris kindly agreed to come and support my efforts to be an MP (which sadly failed!). I had heard terrible stories of him being late or turning up on the wrong day, so when I answered the phone at ten to nine that morning, my heart was already in my mouth. I thought I'd covered every organisational base there was to cover, but, oh no, I hadn't. 'Morning, old bean,' chirruped Boris. 'Nearly at the station now.' As the train was due to depart for

Norwich at 9 a.m, I was already worried. 'Where exactly are you, Boris?' I whimpered. 'Just coming into King's Cross now,' came the rather worrying response. Why worrying? Well, he was supposed to be at Liverpool Street. I just about managed not to cry and rapidly created a Plan B. I got him on the train to King's Lynn – a mere ninety-minute drive from my home near North Walsham, and then of course a ninety-minute drive back. Bearing in mind he was due to speak at a lunch for 150 people at 1 p.m., things were not looking good. In the end we managed to go to the glass-making factory, do an interview with North Norfolk Radio and conduct an interview with the local paper in the back of the car without too much trouble. However, it meant we were forty-five minutes late for the lunch.

We walked into the room and I expected to be lynched. But they all stood and cheered, because, frankly, they had never expected him to be on time. 'Good old Boris,' they cried. Only Boris could have got away with it. Meanwhile, I slumped into my chair, a nervous wreck, thinking to myself, 'Never again.'

In 2008, he successfully ousted Ken Livingstone as Mayor of London. Since then he has brought a new energy and unique style of governance to City Hall. As an LBC radio presenter, I have had the pleasure of interviewing Boris on more than a few occasions over the years, and his charm and wit remain to this day. He gives good interview, as they say, even though he has a very annoying habit of never looking you in the eye when you ask him a difficult question. It makes it very difficult to interrupt him, as he well knows. Sometimes

I have had to remind him that an interview consists of me asking a question, with him answering it, rather than him indulging in a monologue.

Boris is underestimated by many of his opponents because they can't comprehend his popular, cross-party appeal. The left try to paint him as an alt-right, populist extremist, when he is nothing of the sort. Just as they misjudged George W. Bush and tried to dismiss him as 'stupid', they are making the same mistake with Boris. They may live to regret it.

Boris was the coalition government's worst critic. He lambasted the government's housing policy as 'social cleansing', went against Conservative policy and called for a referendum on the EU and warned the government to rethink cuts to police numbers in the wake of the London riots. Boris is the darling of the Conservative grassroots and is seen by many as the only man standing up for Conservative values.

When he finished his eight years as Mayor of London, everyone speculated that No. 10 would be his logical next destination. His leading role in the referendum campaign enabled him to announce he wished to succeed David Cameron. But it was not to be and he withdrew from the contest after an incendiary intervention from Michael Gove. To everyone's surprise, Theresa May appointed him Foreign Secretary, giving him the chance to prove himself on a world stage. It's fair to say that despite one or two triumphs, his tenure at the Foreign Office was not seen as a success. Despite that, when he announced his candidacy to succeed Theresa May, Boris Johnson was instantly made the red-hot favourite.

During the 2019 leadership campaign, I spent more time with him than any other journalist or broadcaster. I hosted ten of the sixteen leadership hustings between Johnson and Jeremy Hunt at venues all around the country, culminating in an amazing evening in London in front of 4,500 people. At the first hustings in Birmingham, I was roundly booed by the audience of Tory members for having the temerity to ask him about his private life, in particular the front-page newspaper reports about a row he was supposed to have had with his partner, Carrie Symonds. As the hustings progressed, I became more and more impressed by candidate Johnson. He purveyed such an optimistic message that I found myself being wound in at times.

One incident at the Carlisle hustings will stay with me for a long time. Jeremy Hunt had departed the stage and I was asking Boris Johnson whether he would declare a climate emergency, when I noticed out of the corner of my eye that a helicopter was landing nearby. Boris had also spotted it and blurted out: 'Well, that's a bit embarrassing. I bang on about climate change, and I think that might be my helicopter.' The audience lapped it up and laughed. A minute or two later, I noticed that Jeremy Hunt was getting into his own helicopter. Boris chimed in: 'Why are we all travelling in separate helicopters? One helicopter!' Cue more laughter. As the helicopter took off, a gust of wind blew into the room. I saw Boris look to his right and it was then I realised the whole staging backdrop starting to fall on top of the both of us. I put my hand up to stop it and managed to push it back into position.

Apart from that, what happens on tour with Boris stays on tour.

On 24 July 2019, Boris Johnson became the most powerful Conservative politician in the country when he achieved his lifetime ambition of becoming Prime Minister.

This is the third and biggest incarnation of this book, since the original *Little Book of Boris* was published way back in 2007. My former PA, now a star journalist with the *Sunday Times*, Grant Tucker, helped me compile the second book, *The Bigger Book of Boris*, and for this volume I am delighted to have a co-author, my LBC producer Jakub Szweda, without whom I would not have had the time to meet the very stern deadline given to me by Biteback. Thanks also to another LBC colleague, Henry Riley, for his contribution.

As I finish writing this introduction at the end of July, Boris has been PM for less than a week. I've said quite often over the past few weeks that I expect Boris to be either one of our greatest Prime Ministers or one of the very worst. There are few shades of grey with Boris. He could be Prime Minister for years, or he be the political equivalent of Lady Jane Grey and end up as our shortest-serving premier.

However it turns out for him and the country, it's surely going to be an interesting ride.

Iain Dale
North Norfolk, July 2019

LIFE, LIBERTY AND THE PURSUIT OF POWER

I had so massacred Bach that I became one of the first pupils in years to fail Grade 1 piano, and still I persevered, in spite of the gentle whispering campaign mounted by my piano teacher to persuade me to give up.

On his childhood aspiration to play the piano

I remember there were a lot of teacher strikes just after I finished teacher training college. I actually received a letter from a union asking if I'd like to sign up. I replied, tersely of course, explaining that I certainly would not, that I opposed their strikes and that they could stick their offer… well, you know.

Try as I might, I could not look at an overhead projection of a growth–profit matrix and stay conscious.

Explaining why he quit after a week as a management consultant

That's one for the memoirs.

**On being rescued after he was swept out to sea
while swimming**

Sometime before the end of August, I will grab a week's leave, like a half-starved sea lion snatching an airborne mackerel, and whatever happens that leave will not be taken in some boarding house in Eastbourne. It will not take place in Cornwall or Scotland or the Norfolk Broads. I say stuff Skegness. I say bugger Bognor. I am going to take a holiday abroad.

On refusing to take a holiday in Britain

All the warning we had was a crackling of the alder branches that bend over the Exe, and the stag was upon us. I can see it now, stepping high in the water, eyes rolling, tongue protruding, foaming, antlers streaming bracken and leaves like the hat of some demented old woman, and behind it the sexual, high-pitched yipping of the dogs. You never saw such a piteous or terrible sight…

It was a stellar performance. I may as well give up now and make way for an older man.

**On his father Stanley's appearance on *Have I Got News For You*,
Daily Express, 12 May 2004**

I'm in charge here!

When things on *Have I Got News For You*
threatened to get out of hand

I've got my fingers in several dykes.

Conservative Party conference, 6 October 2004

OK, I said to myself as I sighted the bird down the end of the gun. This time, my fine feathered friend, there is no escape.

Friends, Voters, Countrymen

What we hate, what we fear, is being ignored.

On the fears of MPs, 21 April 2005

I got to page 1,264 of *War and Peace*. It was really hotting up, but unfortunately I lost my copy.

There is no finer subject. I say that without prejudice to other subjects, which you can basically read in your bath.

On the subject of classics, 2005

I lost the job. Well, the honest truth is that this has been embellished… probably by me, in the sense that there were two of us who were taken on as trainees, and this was in the '80s, I think it was the late '80s, and it was him or me who was going to get the job at the end of… eight months or nine months. It was mano-a-mano and of course it was him who got it.

(In fact, rather than failing to beat another trainee to win a permanent position, he was sacked for falsifying a quotation)

I was just chucking these rocks over the garden wall, and I'd listen to this amazing crash from the greenhouse, next door, over in England, as everything I wrote from Brussels was having this amazing, explosive effect on the Tory Party, and it really gave me this, I suppose, rather weird sense of, of power.

On being the Brussels correspondent for the *Telegraph*, speaking on *Desert Island Discs*, 30 October 2005

It is easy to make promises – it is hard work to keep them.

It's economically illiterate. A degree in classics or philosophy can be as valuable as anything else.

In response to claims that students are dropping certain subjects for courses seen as more useful to their careers

Terrible outbreak of afternoon kipping in Henley. Always in their dressing gowns, hard at it.

On siestas

The trouble with campaigning in the wilds of Oxfordshire is that you lose touch with the main battle. I feel lost in the jungle, way up the Nong River, seventy-five clicks beyond the Do Long bridge.

We are tiny blobs of flesh and blood crawling on the thin integument of a sphere of boiling rock and metal.

On the human race

The royal family are living memorials, the history of the country written in their DNA, a bit like the inscriptions on the Menin Gate. Unlike the Menin Gate, thanks to human reproduction, those genes can go on for ever.

One man's Mickey Mouse course is another man's literae humaniores.

Discussing the 'lite' courses studied at British universities

We seem to have forgotten that societies need rich people, even sickeningly rich people, and not just to provide jobs for those who clean swimming pools and resurface tennis courts.

Lend Me Your Ears

What is a gaffe? A gaffe is in the eye of the beholder.

Wall Street Journal, 3 January 2009

We have the right kind of snow, just the wrong quantity.
Radio 2, 2 February 2009

Piers Morgan: No, you can sit here and take it like a man. You see, I don't really buy into this buffoon thing. I think you play it all up to make money and charm the public, when underneath it all lurks a calculating, ambitious and very serious brain.

Boris Johnson: That's very kind of you, but you must consider the possibility that underneath it all there really may lurk a genuine buffoon.

I'd like thousands of schools as good as the one I went to: Eton.

Great caffeine-powered, keyboard-hammering community of online thinkers who contribute with such richness to the cyberspace jabberama.
On online trolls, 17 January 2011

Come on then, I said to the enemy, just you do that again. Just have another quick look over the top of that empty oil drum, and I am going to give you what for. And then he did, the poor sucker. His head popped up like a meerkat and pow-pow-pow I sent down the rain of death and bam-bam-bam my oily projectiles hit him right where it hurt – or so I assumed.

Everything went quiet. I squinted ahead, and there was a break in the firing. I could hear the breeze in the leaves of this ancient Surrey glade. A pong rose from the puddles ahead. It was time. Like an old cougar plotting his last leap, like Paul Newman at the end of *Butch Cassidy and the Sundance Kid*, I hauled myself forward on my haunches and prepared to explode into the gap ahead. A burst to the left, a burst to the right, and then a Stallone-style roll to the shelter of the next set of drums. That was the plan.

On paintballing, 5 July 2011

Let's skip the dreary, guilt-inducing, afternoon-destroying October lie-in, and let's make the leap into light.

On British Summer Time to be in force all year, *Daily Telegraph,* **31 October 2011**

It is one thing to show solidarity with the Scots by eating porridge for breakfast. But can you really face it on its own? Surely the thing is to add brown sugar or – better still – whorls of golden syrup. If you are like me, you take a childish pleasure in watching as it falls from the spoon, a glistening shaft of solid tawny sunlight.

Daily Telegraph, **12 February 2012**

Gangnam Style is very good. The Prime Minister and I danced Gangnam style the other day, you will be shocked to discover.

Daily Telegraph, **9 October 2012**

Devolution is causing all the strains that its opponents predicted, and in allowing the Scots to make their own laws, while free-riding on English taxpayers, it is simply unjust. The time will come when the Scots will discover that their personal care for the elderly is too expensive, and they will come, cap in hand, to Uncle Sugar in London. And when they do, I propose that we tell them to hop it.

Och aye, it's the New Jerusalem! It's a land of milk and honey they're building up there in Scotland, laddie. They'll nae be doing with your horrid Anglo-Saxon devil-take-the-hindmost approach. No, they're just more socialist than us sour-mouthed Sassenachs.

My life was one of blameless, panda-like passivity until my sister arrived eighteen months later.

BBC documentary, March 2013

Me and my brothers and sisters are like the honey you used to get – produce of more than one country.

BBC documentary, March 2013

[Nigel Farage] has always struck me as a rather engaging geezer.

Daily Telegraph, **28 April 2013**

I'm delighted that as of this autumn any young man will be able to take his chum up the Arsenal … and marry him.

On equal marriage, *Pride of London gala dinner*, **June 2013**

I don't know what a pint of milk costs – so what?

Interview with Jeremy Paxman, 30 September 2013

There is one minority that I still behold with a benign bewilderment, and that is the very, very rich. I mean people who have so much money they can fly by private jet, and who have gin palaces moored in Puerto Banús, and who give their kids McLaren supercars for their eighteenth birthdays and scour the pages of the *FT*'s 'How to Spend It' magazine for jewel-encrusted Cartier collars for their dogs.

I am thinking of the type of people who never wear the same shirt twice, even though they shop in Jermyn Street, and who have other people almost everywhere to do their bidding: people to drive their cars and people to pick up their socks and people to rub their temples with eau de cologne and people to bid for the Munch etching at Christie's.

Please don't get me wrong. I neither resent nor disapprove of such zillionaires; quite the reverse. I just wonder, a bit, what it is like to be so stonkingly rich.

Daily Telegraph, 17 November 2013

One evening not long ago the cat came back in and he was looking pretty washed up. One eye was closed. His leg was gashed. He had internal injuries that were making it more and more difficult for him to move. Finally he sprawled on a chair, in an odd shape, and it was clear that he had been in a serious fight. As his breathing grew fainter, I realised that our cat might die. Then I was seized by a cold and murderous fury. I knew who had done this, and I wanted to pay them back.

When other members of the family have begged for a cat, I have resisted on the grounds that they eat malodorous fishy food and are capable of some dubious smells themselves.

But this evening it was clear that something far worse had happened. It wasn't just the apparently missing eye, and the twisted ear, and the horrible pink cut. There was a rank smell on his fur. It was the smell of his assailant, no question. I could see them in my mind's eye, as I saw them every night: padding insolently across the road in search of someone's rubbish. It was those damn foxes that had attacked our cat, and I was going to sort them out. It was those cruel and cynical canids – and my mind spooled feverishly to fox horror stories: the poor babies gnawed in the crib, the couple who came down to find the decapitated head of their moggie.

Well, they had messed with the wrong cat owner this time. I started to plan the massacre. I knew where they lived, the mangy vermin. We would stalk them in the scrub by the canal, me with the .22 airgun, and another family member with the death-dealing .177. I didn't care what the neighbours said. In fact, I might invite the rest of Islington to form a footpack, so that we could smoke the foxes out of their foul holes and blow them to kingdom come. Or perhaps we could all get up in pink coats and chase them with hounds and fixed-wheel bicycles. Stuff the RSPCA.

Daily Telegraph, 17 November 2013

You have permission to purr.

To Tory Conference delegates, on the NO campaign winning the Scottish independence referendum, 19 September 2014

When asked if he has he gained more respect for the truth as he's got older:

'I… Er… I try to tell the truth in a way that is whole and entire and as clearly as I can and I think that is the secret of, uh, of success in politics and… I think it is Tony Montana in the film *Scarface* who says: 'I always tell the truth even when I lie.'

Interview with Elizabeth Day, *The Observer*, 19 October 2014

Johnson: Uh… I tend to, you know, the time between my head hitting the pillow and being folded in the arms of Morpheus is so short… I don't think I think about anything. I never have any trouble… It's a long time since I've had a… had a sleepless night… I do burn the candle at both ends, so what sleep I get I tend to zonk out pretty firmly, I'm afraid.

When asked what keeps him up at night, Freakonomics.com, November 2014

I can't believe it's that much, it doesn't feel it's that much. Anyway, what's really pathetic is how far behind William Hague I am. What am I doing? I'm earning chicken feed compared to him, I've got to pull my socks up. Even old Winny [Ann Widdecombe] is chasing my tail.

On earning £545,000 in addition to his parliamentary salary, *GQ* magazine, 21 February 2016

I have more in common with a three-toed sloth or a one-eyed pterodactyl or a Kalamata olive than I have with Winston Churchill.

USA Today, 22 February 2016

If someone said, 'You Tory tosser,' I would take it as a badge of honour.

Stephen Dubner: Tell me something you've habitually, throughout your life, spent too much money on but don't regret.

Boris Johnson: Um... Haircuts... I mean, haircuts. Yeah, I spend an awful lot...

SD: Have you ever paid for a haircut?

BJ: No. No, I'm joking. I think I've... I do tend, I do believe that you should try and have good shoes, you know, a decent pair of shoes.

SD: Where do you get your shoes? I'm curious.

BJ: London.

SD: What shop, though, I'm curious.

BJ: Hang on hang on... I think they are...

SD: You're gonna take 'em off?

BJ: No, yeah, hang on... I'm going to take them off...
I'm just going to see if I can see what's in the... These
are so worn... That you can't... Hang on... Uh... Oh
God. Church's!

SD: Oh, Church's, sure!

BJ: Church's! They are Church's shoes. They are very good.

SD: Let me ask you this: what do you collect, if anything, besides old wooden tennis rackets?

BJ: I collect old cheese boxes.

SD: No.

BJ: Old Camembert and Brie ... I love those boxes that
are made of very, very beautifully shaved wood, so that
they have this very smooth texture.

A few years ago, I bought one of those irresistible Christmas presents that you pretend are for the kids, but which you really want to try out yourself. It was a quad bike. To be accurate, it was a mini quad bike. It was superb. In length and breadth it was no bigger than an armchair, but it was full of grunt.

Daily Telegraph, 1 January 2017

I don't know what it is about the Japanese – a lot of raw fish in the diet perhaps – but they do live to prodigious ages. And yes, it is true that my superb Japanese charabanc is now starting to show its antiquity. The exhaust is knackered, so that the car announces its approach like a clanking convict; and at some speeds there is a tapping as though someone has been locked in a forgotten compartment of its capacious interior. My car is so old that I have heard snobbish comments, when stuck in traffic, from other motorists.

Daily Telegraph, 18 October 2018

Asked what his haircare regime is:

Boris Johnson: OK, right. Well, I have no idea.

Elizabeth Day: You must have some notion of what shampoo you use.

BJ: No, I don't! I'm now so short-sighted, I'm blind! My eyes used to be fantastic, but now I cannot actually… There was something in the shower this morning that I used, I cannot honestly tell you what it was. It might have been acne cream. It might have been toothpaste. I honestly couldn't see, but I put it on and it seemed to work.

What is the single worst feature of Christmas? I think it is probably the constant exhortations to be jolly when you may be feeling far from jolly.

Daily Telegraph, 16 December 2018

This country is like a giant that is managing heroically to hop on one leg.

On educational disparities, *Daily Telegraph*, 2 June 2019

I did briefly experiment with veganism. It didn't last. I find it difficult to keep it up for more than six hours at a stretch.

[What broke him?]

I think it was the sheer cruelty of being deprived of cheese. I think I did a couple of days.

The Times, 9 June 2019

I have no embarrassment in confessing that I was one of those kids that made Airfix models. I made planes – Spitfires, Mosquitoes; and I made ships. The floor of my bedroom was turned into an impassable factory as I struggled, wheezing with concentration, to turn hundreds of tiny foot-stabbing plastic components into replicas of great naval vessels. I made HMS *Ark Royal*. I made a tiny HMS *Cossack*; and I remember staring at them in rapture when they were done. I was transported beyond the chaos of Humbrol paints and glue and debris and instructions – and I could see my ships in some storm-tossed Atlantic battle, with enemy torpedoes streaking towards them and fire spouting from their guns.

Daily Telegraph, 7 July 2019

There are many satisfactions in life, but hardly any as intense as making or doing something with your hands – in a way that focuses your entire mind – and then seeing it complete.

Daily Telegraph, 7 July 2019

Yes, it is work that sometimes stresses us out, and work that causes anxiety; but it is also work that can absorb us and take us out of ourselves until the clouds have gone … We can chase away those Black Dogs, boost the economy and save money, all at once.

Daily Telegraph, 14 July 2019

LBC presenter and hustings moderator Iain Dale: Are you good at managing money?

Boris Johnson: I'm... I got into terrible... I think you asked me a question about my personal finances, no, it wasn't you, it was Hannah [Vaughan Jones, previous moderator] who asked me a question. What can I say, I've certainly spent a lot. Yes.

ID: If you're going to be First Lord of the Treasury then you need to be quite good at managing money, I would have thought.

BJ: Yes, I know, but...

Conservative leadership hustings as reported in the *Daily Mail*, 17 July 2019

SEX, LOVE AND AN
INVERTED PYRAMID
OF PIFFLE

There is one measurement I hesitate to mention, since
the last time I did, I am told, the wife of the editor of
The Economist cancelled her subscription to the *Daily
Telegraph* in protest at my crass sexism. It is what is
called the Tottometer, the Geiger counter that detects
good-looking women. In 1997, I reported these were to
be found in numbers at the Labour conference. Now –
and this is not merely my own opinion – the Tories are
fighting back in a big way.

The Spectator, 10 February 2001

Alan Clark... Here was a man, just like the readers of *GQ*, *Esquire*, *Loaded* – all the reassurance-craving magazines that have sprouted in the last ten years – who was endlessly fascinated by the various advantages and disappointments of his own gonads.

I have not had an affair with Petronella. It is complete balderdash. It is an inverted pyramid of piffle. It is all completely untrue and ludicrous conjecture. I am amazed people can write this drivel.

Denying accusations of his having an affair with Petronella Wyatt. *Mail on Sunday*, 7 November 2004

I advise you all very strongly – go for a run, get some exercise and have a beautiful day.

Cornered by reporters asking about his affair after a morning run, 15 November 2004

She was blonde. She was beautiful. She was driving some poxy little Citroen or Peugeot thing… And she had just overtaken me… And let me tell you, I wasn't having it. Because if there is one thing calculated to make the testosterone slosh in your ears like the echoing sea and the red mist of war descend over your eyes, it's being treated as though you were an old woman by a young woman… The whole endocrine orchestra said: 'Go. Take.' You can't be dissed by some blonde in a 305.

On driving an Alfa Romeo

Kate Middleton is not only beautiful, but nice and kind and sweet-natured and charming and hellishly discreet.

18 April 2011

Women cannot resist men who obviously like women.

Voting Tory will cause your wife to have bigger breasts and increase your chances of owning a BMW M3.

I have no idea if I'm a sex symbol.

The book was so ubiquitous that it seemed to speak of some aching need, some lack, some gap in a modern woman's life that we feminist males had never really bargained for.

On *Fifty Shades of Grey*, 23 December 2012

Yes, but mainly asking me to help them with their drains.
On whether he gets lots of female fan mail

Piers Morgan: Are you good in bed?

Boris Johnson: What? I have… I've no idea… No…

PM : Cherie Blair?

BJ: I stick up for her. I think people are too nasty about her. I like her energy.

PM: Do you fancy her?

BJ: Well, erm… I like her. I suppose I… I suppose I do a tiny bit.

When a mighty dam is about to burst it does not just collapse in one explosive roar; it first springs a leak. A jet of water shoots from the crack, and then another crack appears and another horizontal fountain of foam; and as the whole vast curtain of masonry finally begins to tremble the onlookers behold the valley beneath and wonder who and what will be in the path of the billions of pent-up gallons as they are released from their captivity.

So bring on that tide of holy feminist rage and let it wash this horror away.

If you want to solve the problems of the developing world, be a feminist. And if you want to be a feminist, do it by educating girls.

On the #MeToo movement, *Daily Telegraph,* **7 October 2018**

THE NANNY STATE, POLITICAL CORRECTNESS AND BEING RIGHT

Maybe the Tories would do better, and be in a position to act right, if they began by talking left, by explaining the minimal Tory view of the state and society. Because no one looking at the Thatcherites' spending record could be in any doubt: those people thought there was such a thing as society.

There is absolutely no one, apart from yourself, who can prevent you, in the middle of the night, from sneaking down to tidy up the edges of that hunk of cheese at the back of the fridge.

On the dangers of obesity, *Daily Telegraph*, 27 May 2004

Life isn't like coursework, baby. It's one damn essay crisis after another.

In an article titled 'Exams work because they're scary', *Daily Telegraph*, 12 May 2005

If there is one thing wrong with us all these days, it is that we are so mollycoddled, airbagged and swaddled with regulations and protections that we have lost any proper understanding of risk. As long as tobacco is legal, people should be free to balance the pleasures and dangers themselves.

Daily Telegraph, 23 June 2005

I'm very attracted to it. I may be diverting from Tory Party policy here, but I don't care.

On 24-hour drinking legislation

Hypocrisy is at the heart of our national character – without the oil of hypocrisy, the machinery of convention would simply explode.

Daily Telegraph, 15 July 2008

I want now to reassure all smokers that in one way I am on their side. It is precisely my continued failure to take up smoking that leads me to oppose a ban on smoking in public places... Above all, a ban on smoking in public places substitutes the discretion of the state for the individual will, in a way that is morally sapping.

We should be careful, in the current climate, of rushing through legislation that goes too far in expanding the powers of the state. We should beware of eroding our freedoms, when freedom is what we are supposed to be fighting for. O Crime, what liberties are removed in thy name.

We are going to have carnivorous festivals of chops and sausages and burgers and chitterlings and chine and offal, and the fat will run down our chins, and the dripping will blaze on the charcoal, and the smoky vapours will rise to the heavens. We will call these meat feasts Pachauri days, in satirical homage to the tofu-chomping UN man who told the human race to go veggie.

After Dr Rajendra Pachauri, chair of the Intergovernmental Panel on Climate Change, suggested people should give up meat to stop global warming

Ich bin ein Frankfurter.

Uttered while discussing educational freedom

(derived from Felix Frankfurter)

You can continue to believe in the NHS as the sole and
sufficient provider… Or you can conclude that this is
one of the reasons why we have a system which treats
the patients as dolts and serfs…

On the NHS

I object furiously to the element of compulsion, not just because it offends the principles of liberty, but because the whole problem of politics over the past thirty years is that we have proceeded by central legislation rather than leaving decisions to individuals and to communities.

Daily Telegraph, 20 February 2011

I have no idea whether Coca-Cola has a case when it claims that there is absolutely no connection – none whatever! – between kids guzzling sugary drinks and kids getting fat. But what I can say with confidence is that we in Britain have a fatness problem.

Daily Telegraph, 11 June 2012

WIFF-WAFF AND OTHER FORMS OF EXERTION

I love tennis with a passion. I challenged Boris Becker to a match once and he said he was up for it but he never called back. I bet I could make him run around.

Daily Express, 21 March 2005

I'm like a greased panther, a coiled spring, all that suppressed kinetic energy.

Commenting on England *v.* Germany Legends match,

3 May 2006

What I would advise fans is to expect little and possibly they'll receive even less.

Commenting on England *v.* Germany Legends match,

3 May 2006

I used to love the idea of playing football, but whenever I found myself on the pitch, it was like one of those awful dreams where your feet are made of lead and will not move while everyone else is quicksilvering past, and with ever greater desperation you scythe the air with your boot, and you either miss the ball altogether or else you connect with the shins of some other player and over he goes and – peep – you are penalised yet again, or even sent off.

I'm a rugby player, really, and I knew I was going to get to him, and when he was about two yards away I just put my head down. There was no malice. I was going for the ball with my head, which I understand is a legitimate move in soccer.

On his tackle on German midfielder Maurizio Gaudino in a charity football match, May 2006

My hair has yet to induce epilepsy and cost considerably less than £400,000 to design.

When Boris's hair was compared to the new London 2012
Olympic logo, 9 June 2007

We either unleash a full-hearted attack on the nannying, mollycoddling, Harriet Harperson hopelessness of our times, or else too many of our children will grow up fat, unhappy, or violent; we will never win Wimbledon, and football will remain a game in which, in Gary Lineker's immortal words, twenty-two men run around for ninety minutes and then the Germans win.

Daily Telegraph, 1 July 2008

Virtually every single one of our international sports were invented or codified by the British. And I say this respectfully to our Chinese hosts, who have excelled so magnificently at ping-pong. Ping-pong was invented on the dining tables of England in the nineteenth century and it was called wiff-waff!

At the ceremonial passing of the Olympic flag
from China to the UK, 2008

Had it been us staging the Games, I don't think we would necessarily have done the switcheroo with the girl with the braces.

When asked whether he had any criticisms of the Beijing Olympic Games, *The Guardian*, 21 August 2008

I love skiing, and am more or less addicted to the joy of hurling myself down the slopes.

Daily Telegraph, 20 February 2011

Rugby is a fantastic way of letting off steam. At the end of a game of rugby, you sit in the changing room with the relief of one who has just survived being beaten up by the secret police.

29 March 2011

A good dry run for the Olympics.

On the wedding of Prince William and Kate Middleton

It was not only a joy to take the hospitality of the royal box. It was a civic duty.

On his decision to watch the Wimbledon final from the royal box

I have been asked to have a go in it myself but I think it would be electorally inadvisable.

On the Olympic pool

I put down the phone and gazed at the teeming skies. I considered my options. Maybe it was time for prayer. Perhaps we could stage a pagan ritual at Stonehenge, involving either the sacrifice of maidens (if there are any these days), or a goat, or a rabbit, or maybe just a worm – whatever the RSPCA would allow.

Maybe it was time to call upon the sun god Ra, or Phoebus Apollo, or Sol Victrix, or whatever name he now goes by, and lift our hands in chanting entreaty. Come on, O thou fiery spirit that animates the world. Come on out from wherever you are hiding. Shine the light of your countenance upon us, you miserable blighter. Extend thy beams, so reverend and strong, and dry the water from our upturned cheeks. Flatter the mountain tops with your sovereign eye, vaporise the thunderheads, and give us all a break.

Give us poor Britons some kind of a summer – before the entire country dissolves like a sugar cube and sinks into the sea…

Blow, winds and crack your cheeks. Blow, you cataracts and hurricanoes, spout till you have drenched our country yet again. We don't give a monkey's. We like a spot of precipitation. It intensifies the pleasure of the sun. Made us what we are. And by the way, it still rains more in Rome than it does in London.

Daily Telegraph, 16 July 2012

The excitement is growing so much I think the Geiger counter of Olympo-mania is going to go zoink off the scale.

At Hyde Park torch relay party, 26 July 2012

There are semi-naked women playing beach volleyball glistening like wet otters.

On women's beach volleyball at the 2012 Olympic Games,
30 July 2012

Reasons to be cheerful about the way things are going…

1. The Games so far are a particular triumph for British women, and for female emancipation in general. It was great to see that female judo competitor from Saudi Arabia – the first in history. She may have got squashed, but Saudi women will never look back.

2. In fact, the whole business is encouraging us all to get in touch with our feminine side. Athletes, spectators, politicians – we are all blubbing like Andy Murray on a bad day. Can you blame us? Go on – let it all out. There, there, feeling better? Blow your nose on this.

Daily Telegraph, 6 August 2012

Well, as things have turned out I reckon we have knocked Beijing – with all respect to our Chinese friends, and greatly though I admired those Games – into a cocked hat.

On the 2012 Olympics, *Daily Telegraph*, 13 August 2012

And then sometime in that first week it was as though a giant hormonal valve had been opened in the minds of the people. And the endorphins seemed to flow through the crowds. And down the Tube trains like some benign contagion.

Conservative Party conference, 2012

SELF-KNOWLEDGE IS A WONDERFUL THING

[I am] a wise guy playing the fool to win.
Sunday Times, 16 July 2000

Vote Johnson, vote often – there is a ready supply of Johnsons waiting to step into whatever breaches are left in whatever constituencies.

Boris while out visiting his dad's Teignbridge constituency, 2005

I'm kicking off my diet with a cheeseburger – whatever Jamie Oliver says, McDonald's are incredibly nutritious and, as far as I can tell, crammed full of vital nutrients and rigid with goodness.

While campaigning at McDonald's in Botley, Oxford, May 2005

I've always known my life would be turned into a farce. I'm just glad it's been entrusted to two such distinguished men of letters.

On discovering that Toby Young and Lloyd Evans had written a play about his sex life, 2005

I can hardly condemn UKIP as a bunch of boss-eyed, foam-flecked euro hysterics, when I have been sometimes not far short of boss-eyed, foam-flecked hysteria myself. My speaking style was criticised by no less an authority than Arnold Schwarzenegger. It was a low moment, my friends, to have my rhetorical skills denounced by a monosyllabic Austrian cyborg.

THE YELLOW PERIL

There are not many Lib Dems in Parliament, but even in that tiny group they incarnate dozens of diametrically opposing positions. You want to know what the Lib Dem policy is on taxation, for instance, and you want to know whether they are for or against a 50 per cent tax rate. One half of your cerebrum thinks it is quite right that the rich should pay more; the other lobe thinks tax is quite high enough already. You are a perfect Lib Dem, a mass of contradictions, and your party supplies exactly what you are looking for.

Their policy on cake is pro-having it and pro-eating it.

Discussing Liberal Democrat policies

The Lib Dems are not just empty. They are a void within a vacuum surrounded by a vast inanition.

They are a bunch of euro-loving road-hump fetishists who are attempting like some defective vacuum cleaner to suck and blow at the same time.

Daily Telegraph, 19 April 2010

So in the dwindling months we have available, it is time for us Clegg fans to echo those kindly folk who are trying to save the sweet furry badgers from the wrath of farmers. Never mind the badgers – save the Cleggster from extermination!

Daily Telegraph, 24 September 2012

Lib Dems are wobbling jellies of indecision and vacillation, particularly Clegg.

Huffington Post, 20 February 2013

On Nick Clegg: I don't want to cast aspersions on my fellow, err... What is he... He's a radio disc jockey now, isn't he? I'm sure he has many, many important ceremonial duties. He is a sort of lapdog of David Cameron who's been converted by taxidermy into a kind of protective shield, like the Emperor Valerian who was skinned and hung on the wall. That's what he reminds me of. He is a very, very decorative part of the constitution. Insofar as he fulfils any function at all, it is to stop sensible policy being promulgated by this government, as far as I can make out. That's basically what he does. The sooner we are shot of the great yellow albatross, in my view, the better.

ITV News, 13 December 2013

[Clegg] is a kind of shield. He's a lapdog who's been skinned and turned into a shield.

The Guardian, 8 January 2014

I am absolutely amazed to hear that the Liberal Democrats could take two positions at once on anything. It is quite an astonishing revelation.

16 March 2016

CYCLING AND OTHER INFERIOR FORMS OF TRANSPORTATION

No one obeys the speed limit except a motorised rickshaw.

Daily Telegraph, 12 July 2001

Nor do I propose to defend the right to talk on a mobile while driving a car, though I don't believe that is necessarily any more dangerous than the many other risky things that people do with their free hands while driving – nose-picking, reading the paper, studying the A–Z, beating the children and so on.

1 August 2002

I forgot that to rely on a train, in Blair's Britain, is to engage in a crapshoot with the devil ... A horse is a safer bet than the trains.

Daily Telegraph, 3 July 2003

We need to end the appalling tendency of the present Livingstone regime in City Hall to treat fare-dodging as a kind of glorious Che Guevara two-fingers to the capitalist conspiracy.

On fare-dodging under Ken Livingstone

The M3 opened up before me, a long quiet Bonneville flat stretch, and I am afraid it was as though the whole county of Hampshire was lying back and opening her well-bred legs to be ravished by the Italian stallion.

On driving a Ferrari

[On test driving a Nissan Murano] 'Tee hee,' I said to myself as I took in the ludicrously arrogant Darth Vader-style snout. What was it saying, with the plutocratic sneer of that gleaming grille?

It was saying, 'Out of my way, small car driven by ordinary person on modest income. Make way for Murano!'

Life in the Fast Lane

You should not underestimate my militant determination to increase cycling.

New Statesman, 26 February 2010

In 1904, 20 per cent of journeys were made by bicycle in London. I want to see a figure like that again. If you can't turn the clock back to 1904, what's the point of being a Conservative?

At the Barclays Cycle hire launch, 30 July 2010

I ploughed repeatedly into the grass. I took out one of the runway lights. I span like a bar of soap on a wet bathroom floor, and my course was so unpredictable, I was informed, that there was some risk to the health and safety of the camera crews.

On his *Top Gear* appearance

I was cycling through central London the other day when my heart lurched. There it was – in its natural habitat. I felt the surge of excitement that I imagine you must get on safari, when after days of scanning the veld you finally see a representative of some species of charismatic megafauna. I could tell instantly what it was: I recognised the noble curve of the brow, like a bowler hat or an African elephant.

On the Routemaster bus, *Daily Telegraph*, 19 March 2012

As we speak, as we speak, beneath the streets of London are six colossal boring machines called Ada and Phyllis and Mary and Elizabeth and Victoria, I think, I have got their names wrong, I can't remember their names, but they all have female names for some reason and Phyllis and Ada are coming in from the west and Mary and Elizabeth are going from the east, from the Limmo Peninsula, and they are chomping remorselessly through the London clay and they are going to meet somewhere around Whitechapel for this ginormous convocation of worms – I don't know what they'll do but it will be absolutely terrific because the rail capacity of London will be increased by 10 per cent and we will have done Crossrail, I confidently predict, as we did the Olympics, on time and on budget.

On Crossrail, Conservative Party conference, 5 October 2013

We must not go back to the old failed Labour idea of a third runway at Heathrow. You knew I was going to say this, but I'm going to say it, a third runway at Heathrow aggravating noise pollution in what is already the city in the world worst affected by noise pollution by miles. It was Ed Balls's idea, I seem to remember, back in the days when Labour were in power, it is Ed Balls's idea now. It was Balls then, it's Balls now and it is not good enough for this country, it isn't the right answer for the most beautiful and liveable city on earth.

On a third runway at Heathrow, Conservative Party conference, 5 October 2013

After more than fifteen years of daily cycling in London, I have tasted the air in all weathers and at all hours of the day and night. I have sampled the vapours of every vehicle and every animal on our streets. Stationary and powerless I have waited behind buses. I have heard them wheeze like wounded war elephants, and seen the dreadful shudder of their flanks. I have watched the consumptive coughing from their tail-pipes, and I have seen the atmosphere turn palpably brown around the rear ends – thick, brown, and as full of lethal carcinogens as some chemical factory in the former Soviet Union.

Daily Telegraph, 6 April 2014

Why don't you fuck off and die, why don't you fuck off and die – and not in that order.

Huffington Post, 5 June 2015 [London Mayor, MP and vaunted future Prime Minister Boris Johnson was involved in a testy exchange with a cabbie. The video was captured on a mobile phone by an onlooker and subsequently peddled to *The Sun*. According to the report, the driver had accused Boris of failing to protect the capital's traditional black cabs, which have suffered from competition from app-based companies such as Uber.]

Asked whether he had ever done anything illegal, Johnson again avoided mentioning drugs and said: I cannot swear that I have always observed a top speed limit of 70 mph.

Metro, 12 June 2019

THE LONG ARM
OF THE LAW

Yes, cannabis is dangerous, but no more than other perfectly legal drugs. It's time for a rethink, and the Tory party – the funkiest, most jiving party on Earth – is where it's happening.

Daily Telegraph, 12 July 2001

I was at this party in Islington the other day and we were all glugging back the champagne, and suddenly I could resist it no longer. The urge rose within me, as though some genie had seized the diaphragm. 'Hague,' I roared. 'Haguey! Don't you think he's absolutely right to say this stuff about crime? Isn't he spot on?' And their eyes bulged like the very crustaceans on the canapés.

Defending William Hague's tough stance on crime

What's my view on drugs? I've forgotten my view on drugs.

On the campaign trail in the 2005 general election

I think I was once given cocaine but I sneezed so it didn't go up my nose. In fact, it may have been icing sugar.

Evening Standard, 17 October 2005

Piers Morgan: Have you ever tried any other drugs?

Boris Johnson: Any dope? Cannabis, you mean? Yes, I have.

PM: How many spliffs?

BJ: There was a period before university when I had quite a few. But funnily enough, not much at university.

PM: Did it do much for you?

BJ: Ummmm. Yeah, it was jolly nice. But apparently it is very different these days. Much stronger. I've become very illiberal about it. I don't want my kids to take drugs.

ON THE POLICE

A cynic would say that they were all stuck on racial awareness programmes; or deployed in desperate attempts to catch paedophiles in ancient public schools; or lurking in lay-bys in the hope of penalising a motorist; or perhaps preparing for the great moment when they will be able to arrest anyone who allows his dogs to chase rabbits, let alone those who go foxhunting.

When you see a mugging on Holloway Road, and the villain scarpers into the night, there's no point looking around for a policeman. But in due course the police turn up in a high-powered car, and you are ferried with flashing lights, up and down, up and down – in a macho Starsky and Hutch display that has become utterly banal – while the mugger has melted away.

This is not a time to think about making substantial cuts in police numbers.

After the London riots of 2011

The chief constables originally had good reasons for thinking that it was a waste of manpower to have men in uniform pounding the pavements, or cycling through tranquil villages. Their men were likely to stumble across a robbery in progress, on average, once every eight years. What the chiefs forgot is the psychological effect of denuding the streets of coppers. There is a sense of lawlessness around, and insolent impunity. As for those policemen who are still on the beat, they have plenty of excuse for feeling assailed by this government.

Soft is the perfect way to enjoy French cheese, but not how we should approach punishing criminals.

It is a cynical attempt to pander to the many who think the world would be a better place if dangerous folk with dusky skins were just slammed away, and never mind a judicial proceeding.

On the dangers of the 2005 Prevention of Terrorism Bill

ON THE INTRODUCTION OF CONTROL ORDERS

Are you really telling me that it is a sensible ordering of priorities to round up Twitter-borne transphobes and chuck them in the clink, when violence on the streets would seem to be getting out of control?

Daily Telegraph, 10 January 2019

Keeping numbers high on the streets is certainly important. But it depends where you spend the money and where you deploy the officers. And one comment I would make is I think an awful lot of money and an awful lot of police time now goes into these historic offences and all this malarkey. You know, £60 million I saw being spaffed up the wall on some investigation into historic child abuse.

LBC interview with Nick Ferrari, 13 March 2019

JOHNNY FOREIGNER

It is said that the Queen has come to love the Commonwealth, partly because it supplies her with regular cheering crowds of flag-waving piccaninnies; and one can imagine that Blair, twice victor abroad but enmired at home, is similarly seduced by foreign politeness. They say he is shortly off to the Congo. No doubt the AK47s will fall silent, and the pangas will stop their hacking of human flesh, and the tribal warriors will all break out in watermelon smiles to see the big white chief touch down in his big white British taxpayer-funded bird.

Daily Telegraph, 10 January 2002

The problem is not that we were once in charge, but that we are not in charge any more … Consider Uganda, pearl of Africa, as an example of the British record … the British planted coffee and cotton and tobacco, and they were broadly right … If left to their own devices, the natives would rely on nothing but the instant carbohydrate gratification of the plantain. You never saw a place so abounding in bananas: great green barrel-sized bunches, off to be turned into matooke. Though this dish (basically fried banana) was greatly relished by Idi Amin, the colonists correctly saw that the export market was limited … The best fate for Africa would be if the old colonial powers, or their citizens, scrambled once again in her direction; on the understanding that this time they will not be asked to feel guilty.

Discussing his views on Africans and 'Instant Carbohydrate Gratification', *The Spectator*, 2 February 2002

If this is war, let's win it. Let's fly with whatever it takes to the mountain eyrie of Bin Laden, winkle him out, and put him on trial. If we can find good evidence that he is guilty, and he puts up any resistance, then let's not even bother with the judicial process. Let's find the scum who did this and wipe them off the face of the Earth.

Now, there will be plenty of British Conservatives who think these Taliban chappies run a tight ship, women's lib is not an unalloyed blessing, look at all these poofters these days, and so on. There are even ex-feminists, such as Germaine Greer, who will take a perverse pleasure in announcing that women can look very beautiful in a veil.

Chinese cultural influence is virtually nil, and unlikely to increase ... Indeed, high Chinese culture and art are almost all imitative of Western forms: Chinese concert pianists are technically brilliant, but brilliant at Schubert and Rachmaninov. Chinese ballerinas dance to the scores of Diaghilev. The number of Chinese Nobel Prizes won on home turf is zero, although there are of course legions of bright Chinese trying to escape to Stanford and Caltech ... The Chinese have a script so fiendishly complicated that they cannot produce a proper keyboard for it.

Have I Got Views for You

When I look at the streets of London, I see a future for the planet, a model of cooperation and harmony between races and religions, in which barriers are broken down by tolerance, humour and respect – without giving way either to bigotry, or to the petty balkanisation of the race relations industry.

July 2007

The two men look vaguely similar; they both appear to believe in the efficacy of Grecian 2000; they both favour long and rambling speeches on socialist economic and political theory, with Col. Gaddafi's efforts perhaps having a slight edge in logic and coherence.

Boris comparing Gordon Brown to Colonel Gaddafi, 28 February 2011

I hope and believe that Gaddafi's days are now numbered, and that he will either fall victim to the lead-weighted handkerchief in the bunga-bunga tent or else be issued with a one-way ticket to Venezuela, where he can live out his retirement, like other fallen socialists, as a consultant to the regime of Hugo Chávez.

On Gaddafi's future

Whatever happens in the world, whatever the catastrophe, we approach it like some vast BBC reporter with an addiction to the first person singular. We just have to put ourselves at the centre of the story.

After the Japanese tsunami, 14 March 2011

We have created a multi-cultural society that has many beauties and attractions, but in which too many Britons have absolutely no sense of allegiance to this country or its institutions. It is a cultural calamity that will take decades to reverse and we must begin now with what I call the re-Britannification of Britain.

Inventing new words

Wherever he is I wager there is one thing that causes the old dyed ringlets to shake with rage, one thought that brings the foam to the corner of his champing jaws – and that is the treachery of all those he thought of as friends. And of those who have ratted on him in the last six months, there is one particular group of traitors that he would like to cast – I bet – to the nethermost fire-bubbling pit of hell. Never mind the rebels, and all those snaky ex-ministers who chose to defect as soon as the going got tough. Forget the buxom female 'bodyguards' who took the first plane back to Ukraine. For sheer duplicity there is no one to beat – the British! May the fleas of a thousand camels infest their armpits!

Gaddafi groans behind his dark glasses, pouring some hot sauce on the falafel.

Daily Telegraph, 5 September 2011

There is one overarching philosophy behind everything we do in City Hall that can be traced to a saying of Mahatma Gandhi, who prophesied in 1948 that the future of India lay in its 700,000 villages. As anyone who has been to India can testify, Gandhi was wrong.

New Statesman, 4 October 2011

Boris was appearing at the Forum alongside Malaysian Prime Minister Najib Razak, talking about the role of women in Islamic societies. When Razak commented that 'Before coming here my officials told me that of the latest university intake in Malaysia, a Muslim country, 68 per cent will be women,' Boris cut him off by quipping: 'They've got to find men to marry.'

Cosmopolitan, 8 July 2013

I cannot think of anything more foolish than to say you want to have any kind of divestment or sanctions or boycott against a country that, when all is said and done, is the only democracy in the region, is the only place that has, in my view, a pluralist open society.

Why boycott Israel? And by the way I think there is some misunderstanding over here about it. The supporters of this so-called boycott are really a bunch of, you know, corduroy-jacketed academics.

They are by and large lefty academics who have no real standing in the matter and I think are highly unlikely to be influential on Britain. This is a very, very small minority in our country who are calling for this.

On a boycott of Israeli goods, Huffington Post, 10 November 2015

Despite looking a bit like Dobby the House Elf, he is a ruthless and manipulative tyrant.

On Vladimir Putin, *Daily Telegraph*, 6 December 2015

Hooray, I say. Bravo – and keep going. Yes, I know. Assad is a monster, a dictator. He barrel-bombs his own people. His jails are full of tortured opponents. He and his father ruled for generations by the application of terror and violence – and yet there are at least two reasons why any sane person should feel a sense of satisfaction at what Assad's troops have accomplished.

On the saving of Palmyra, *Daily Telegraph*, 27 March 2016

I am a child of Europe. I am a liberal cosmopolitan and my family is a genetic UN peacekeeping force.

***The Independent*, 9 May 2016**

Global trade is not carried on by kind permission of people like Peter Mandelson. People and businesses trade with each other, and always will, as long as they have something to buy and sell.

ConservativeHome, 9 May 2016

Winner of *The Spectator*'s President Erdogan Offensive Poetry competition:

> There was a young fellow from Ankara,
> Who was a terrific wankerer.
> Till he sowed his wild oats,
> With the help of a goat,
> But he didn't even stop to thankera.

The Spectator, 18 May 2016

Life expectancy in Africa has risen astonishingly as that country has entered the global economic system.

Calling Africa 'that country', 2 October 2016

They have got a brilliant vision to turn Sirte into the next Dubai. The only thing they have got to do is clear the dead bodies away.

On the future of Libya, BBC, 3 October 2017

[The attack was] a sign [from President Putin that] no one could escape the long arm of Russian revenge … [The attack] was a sign that President Putin or the Russian state wanted to give to potential defectors in their own agencies: this is what happens to you if you decide to support a country with a different set of values. You can expect to be assassinated.

On the Skripal poisoning, BBC News, 21 March 2018

If you do that, you have to answer the question: what next? What if the Iranians do rush for a nuclear weapon? Are we seriously saying that we are going to bomb those facilities at Fordo and Natanz? Is that really a realistic possibility? Or do we work round what we have got and push back on Iran together?

On Trump and the Iran nuclear deal, BBC News, 7 May 2018

It is often immigrants who like waving flags and receiving CBEs, and they certainly seem pretty good at cricket.

Discussing the pros and cons of British immigration

There seems no reason to behave respectfully towards that little old woman coming out of the Post Office if you feel that she belongs to a culture that is alien from your own ... Why not piss against the wall if you feel that it is not really your wall, but part of a foreign country.

Lend Me Your Ears

We are the only country in the world to have a trade surplus with America in music. And our manufacturing ingenuity gets daily more boggling. I think of the Uxbridge factory that makes bus stops in Las Vegas. Wake up with a hangover in Vegas and the chances are that a little piece of London is shielding you from the elements. And the other Uxbridge factory that makes the futuristic wooden display cabinets for duty-free Toblerones in every airport in Saudi Arabia. Think of that – the invisible hand of the market circling the earth in search of a Toblerone cabinet and pointing at Uxbridge.

Conservative Party conference, 2 October 2018

I'm not a nationalist if by that you mean I'm a xenophobe or someone who deprecates other countries and cultures. Absolutely not, far from it. I'm called Boris, apart from anything else.

Daily Mirror, 19 January 2019

It is a matter of economic fact that, when Vladimir Putin says that liberalism is obsolete, he is talking the most tremendous tripe … To put it simply, if your property can be arbitrarily confiscated by the wife of the president, or by his son-in-law, then you won't start a business in that country and you won't invest.

Daily Telegraph, 30 June 2019

WHERE ANGELS FEAR
TO TREAD

Some readers will no doubt say that a devil is inside me; and though my faith is a bit like Magic FM in the Chilterns, in that the signal comes and goes, I can only hope that isn't so.

Daily Telegraph, 4 March 2004

It is no use the Muslim Council of Great Britain endlessly saying that 'the problem is not Islam', when it is blindingly obvious that in far too many mosques you can find sermons of hate, and literature glorifying 9/11 and vilifying Jews.

Daily Telegraph, 14 July 2005

The proposed ban on incitement to 'religious hatred' makes no sense unless it involves a ban on the Koran itself.

Daily Telegraph, 21 July 2005

When is *Little Britain* going to do a sketch starring Matt Lucas as one of the virgins? Islam will only be truly acculturated to our way of life when you could expect a Bradford audience to roll in the aisles at Monty Python's Life of Mohammed.

The other day I was giving a pretty feeble speech when it went off the cliff and became truly abysmal. It was at some kind of founder's dinner for a university, and I had badly miscalculated my audience. I thought it was going to be a bunch of students, and when I saw the elite group of retired generals, former *Telegraph* editors and Nobel Prize-winning economists, all in black tie, with their wives, I desperately tried to extemporise something profound. There were some musty sepulchres set into the wall of the ancient hall, so I started burbling about social mobility in the eighteenth century and widening participation in universities today. Frankly, I thought my sermon was more or less ideal. I began some guff-filled sentence with the words, 'I am sure we all agree...' It seemed to go well, so I did it again. 'I am sure we all agree we need world-class skills...', I said, or something equally banal, at which point a man down the table shot to his feet and shouted, 'Well, I don't! I don't agree with what you are saying at all. It seems to me to be quite wrong for you to claim that we all agree when I don't agree.' And blow me down, he appeared to be wearing long purple vestments. It was, of course, Britain's most turbulent priest, the Bishop of Southwark. I realised I was being heckled by a blooming bishop, and from that moment on my speech was irretrievable. I told a long and rambling story about sheep, in the hope that the man of God would be appeased, and sat down. I did sniff him later on, and though there was an aroma of hot cassock he didn't seem notably drunk.

The Spectator, 27 January 2007

I would go further and say that it is absolutely ridiculous that people should choose to go around looking like letter boxes. If a female student turned up at school or at a university lecture looking like a bank robber then ditto: those in authority should be allowed to converse openly with those that they are being asked to instruct.

Daily Telegraph, 5 August 2018

BUSINESS, ECONOMICS
AND NUMBERS

If the fuel strikers had not struck, people would never have grasped so clearly how much money Gordon is filching. It is thanks to the fuel protesters that we understand what a regressive tax it is, and how it has helped the tax burden of the poorest fifth of society to rise by 3 per cent since 1997. It is thanks to the fuel strikers that tax and public spending are now again at the centre of politics. Blair will say he can't cut taxes because it is inflationary, or because he needs to spend the money on pensions, or schools or hospitals. He can't have it both ways. We need to remember that we can't compete endlessly with other nations that set their income taxes substantially lower than ours. They will attract jobs, and investment. They may generate more tax – and they may even persuade their tennis champs to run that extra half yard.

September 2000

Not even Mr Blair has been able to erode the union's conviction that we all have a 'right' to a minimum wage ... Both the minimum wage and the Social Charter would palpably destroy jobs.

Lend Me Your Ears

We should never forget that in asking people to vote for us we are essentially asking to take charge of taxation and spending, and that our prime duty is to bring a new and more sensible – and more Conservative – style of economic management ... The public sector is continuing to expand, and Brown is taking ever more money from the private sector to fund this expansion, and therefore preventing its use in wealth creation or the generation of new jobs.

Have I Got Views For You

I rubbed my eyes and emitted a sigh as tragic as Prince Charles on beholding the blueprints for the Gherkin.

Daily Telegraph, 15 July 2008

Tesco the destroyer of the old-fashioned high street, Tesco the slayer of small shops, Tesco through whose air-conditioned portals we are all sucked like chaff, as though hypnotised by some Moonie spell.

Daily Telegraph, 15 July 2008

Reward them for what? You might as well give Lord Cardigan a bonus for the Charge of the Light Brigade.

On bankers' bonuses

Comrades, I have the solution. I have an export-led answer to Britain's current economic difficulties. We need to export Ed Miliband to China. We need to send Ed Balls to India and all the rest of the Labour lot to the Asian, Latin American and African countries that are currently outperforming the UK.

Daily Telegraph, 3 October 2011

The harder you shake the pack, the easier it will be for some cornflakes to get to the top. And for one reason or another – boardroom greed or, as I am assured, the natural and god-given talent of boardroom inhabitants – the income gap between the top cornflakes and the bottom cornflakes is getting wider than ever … To get back to my cornflake packet, I worry that there are too many cornflakes who aren't being given a good enough chance to rustle and hustle their way to the top.

Speech to the Centre for Policy Studies, November 2013

Plato said no one should earn more than five times anyone else. Well, Plato would have been amazed by the growth in corporate inequality today. In 1980 the multiple was twenty-five. By 1998 it had risen to forty-seven. After ten years of Tony Blair and Peter Mandelson – and their 'intensely relaxed' attitude to getting 'filthy rich' – the top executives of big UK firms were earning 120 times the average pay of the shop floor. Last year it was 130 times.

Daily Telegraph, 15 May 2016

But when I mentioned another priority of mine – almost casually – those farmers smote their weather-beaten hands together and roared their assent. They want better broadband.

On speaking to Lincolnshire Conservatives, *Daily Telegraph*, 23 June 2018

There are whole towns in Britain where people are still being driven wild with frustration as they stare at the slowly revolving pizza wheel of doom.

Daily Telegraph, 23 June 2018

I am a mild-mannered man. It takes a lot to get my goat. But when an Uxbridge constituent showed me around his new family home, I thought I was about to blow a gasket.

On the quality of new-build houses, *Daily Telegraph*,
12 August 2018

When the LBC radio host Nick Ferrari said chief executive of Jaguar Land Rover Ralf Speth knew more about car manufacturing than Johnson: 'Well actually, it's an interesting point. I'm not certain he does, by the way.'

The Guardian, **14 January 2019**

THE FERAL BEAST

We are confident in our story and will be fighting this all the way. I am very sorry that Alastair Campbell has taken this decision but I can see that he got his tits in the wringer.

On Alastair Campbell's negative reply to *The Spectator*'s report that the government had influenced the Queen Mother's funeral arrangements

I don't see why people are so snooty about Channel 5. It has some respectable documentaries about the Second World War. It also devotes considerable airtime to investigations into lap dancing, and other related and vital subjects.

Daily Telegraph, 14 March 2002

I didn't see it, but it sounds barbaric. It's become like cock-fighting: poor dumb brutes being set upon each other by conniving television producers.

On *Big Brother*, reported in *The Observer*, 20 June 2004

[I have been propelled] as a fat German tourist may be transported by superior alpinists to the summit of Everest.

Praising colleagues at *The Spectator* in his leaving speech, December 2005

Polly Toynbee ... incarnates all the nannying, high-taxing, high-spending, schoolmarminess of Blair's Britain. She is the defender and friend of everyone whose non-job has ever been advertised in the *Guardian* appointments page, every gay and lesbian outreach worker, every clipboard-toter and pen-pusher and form-filler whose function has been generated by mindless regulation. Polly is the high priestess of our paranoid, mollycoddled, risk-averse, airbagged, booster-seated culture of political correctness and 'elf 'n' safety fascism.

Daily Telegraph, 23 November 2006

Mr Blobby and Beethoven are yokemates of broadcasting destiny.

16 September 2008

Get rid of the licence fee and you lose the vast red velvet drapes in the Albert Hall saying BBC Proms; and without the BBC Proms there would have been no frenzied Italian conductor, his spasms barely contained by the polished brass of the stand.

On the licence fee, 16 September 2008

One of the great things about journalism is that if you are in doubt about what to write there is always space for knocking copy – and the more popular and well-loved the topic of your piece, the more acute the demand for someone who is willing to step up and put the boot in.

18 April 2011

It is possible to have a pretty good life and career being a leech and a parasite in the media world, gadding about from TV studio to TV studio, writing inconsequential pieces and having a good time. But in the end you have a great sense of personal dissatisfaction.

Spending an hour with the *FT* is like being trapped in a room with assorted members of a millennialist suicide cult. If their pundits are to be believed, the skies of the City will shortly be dark with falling bankers, and then for the rest of us it's back to the 1930s, with barrels for trousers, soup kitchens and buddy can you spare a dime.

Daily Telegraph, 14 October 2011

THE STAR-SPANGLED BANNER

Not only did I want Bush to win, but we threw the entire weight of *The Spectator* behind him.

Lend Me Your Ears

That is the best case for Bush; that, among other things, he liberated Iraq. It is good enough for me.

Daily Telegraph, 26 February 2004

You know, whenever George Dubya Bush appears on television, with his buzzard squint and his Ronald Reagan side-nod, I find a cheer rising irresistibly in my throat. Yo, Bush baby, I find myself saying, squashing my beer can like some crazed red-neck. You tell 'em boy. Just you tell all those pointy-headed liberals where to get off.

Lend Me Your Ears

One moment he might be holding forth to a great per-spiring tent at Hay-on-Wye. The next moment, click, some embarrassed member of the Welsh constabulary could walk on stage, place some handcuffs on the former leader of the Free World, and take him away to be charged. Of course, we are told this scenario is un-likely. Dubya is the former leader of a friendly power, with whom this country is determined to have good relations. But that is what torture-authorising Augusto Pinochet thought. And unlike Pinochet, Mr Bush is making no bones about what he has done.

Warning that George W. Bush could be arrested if he visits the UK

She's got dyed blonde hair and pouty lips, and a steely blue stare, like a sadistic nurse in a mental hospital.

On Hillary Clinton, *Daily Telegraph*, 1 November 2007

Unlike the current occupant of the White House, he has no difficulty in orally extemporising a series of grammatical English sentences, each containing a main verb.

Endorsing Barack Obama, *Daily Telegraph*, 21 October 2008

We are still the second most important country on Earth. The trick of maintaining such influence, of course, is to go around pretending to be very bumbling and hopeless and self-deprecating, a skill at which we excel.

I could be president of the United States, technically speaking.

Daily Telegraph, 7 June 2012

I don't want to risk polonium in my sushi by bandying statistics with the Kremlin about per capital GDP or life expectancy except to say that the UK of course vastly exceeds Russia in both. The reason so many Russians come here is that they recognise that London is not simply the capital of Britain but also of the EU and, in many ways, of the world. A city with more American banks in it than there are in New York, for heaven's sake. A 24-hour city in which there are 100,000 people working in supplying us all with coffee in the coffee bars of London, how about that? We have more baristas than barristers, there are quite a few barristers as well, and yet with so much green space in London that we produce 2 million cucumbers a year from London. Eat your heart out, Vladimir Putin.

Conservative Party conference, 5 October 2013

Crime has been falling steadily both in London and in New York – and the only reason I wouldn't go to some parts of New York is the real risk of meeting Donald Trump. He is betraying a quite stupefying ignorance that makes him frankly unfit to hold the office of President of the United States.

On Trump's comment about 'no-go areas' of London,

9 December 2015

I would invite him to come and see the whole of London and take him round the city, except that I wouldn't want to expose any Londoners to any unnecessary risk of meeting Donald Trump.

9 December 2015

I think Donald Trump is clearly out of his mind if he thinks that's a sensible way to proceed, you can't ban people going to the US in that way, or to any country.

On the presidential candidate's suggestion that Muslims should be banned from entering the US, 9 December 2015

Something mysterious happened when Barack Obama entered the Oval Office in 2009. Something vanished from that room, and no one could quite explain why. It was a bust of Winston Churchill – the great British war time leader. It was a fine goggle-eyed object, done by the brilliant sculptor Jacob Epstein, and it had sat there for almost ten years. But on day one of the Obama administration it was returned, without ceremony, to the British embassy in Washington. No one was sure whether the President had himself been involved in the decision. Some said it was a snub to Britain. Some said it was a symbol of the part-Kenyan President's ancestral dislike of the British empire – of which Churchill had been such a fervent defender … Some said that perhaps Churchill was seen as less important than he once was. Perhaps his ideas were old-fashioned and out of date. Well, if that's why Churchill was banished from the Oval Office, they could not have been more wrong.

The Mayor of London penned a piece in *The Sun* attacking President Obama for urging Britain to stay in the EU, 22 April 2016

The first time Donald Trump tried to call Boris Johnson for a chat, Johnson assumed it was a hoax. He took a call from someone purporting to be the Downing Street switchboard:

The person had a mild Irish accent and said, 'This is the No. 10 switchboard, we have got the President of the United States for you. I am just going to patch you through to the White House situation room.' Thinking quickly as I do, I said, 'To all our listeners on Radio Kilkenny, I was not fooled for an instant.' [Johnson hung up and dialled No. 10.] And indeed it was the President.

On his first phone call with Donald Trump

If he can fix North Korea and if he can fix the Iran nuclear deal, then I don't see why he's any less of a candidate for a Nobel Peace Prize than Barack Obama, who got it before he even did anything.

On Donald Trump, *Washington Post*, 7 May 2018

MAYOR OF THE GREATEST CITY IN THE WORLD

If you ask me my vision for London, let me say that one of the most important things I want is a city where Jacqui Smith feels safe enough to pop out and buy a kebab – at any time of day or night.

17 February 2008

Look, I wouldn't trust Harriet Harman's political judgement.

When told that Harriet Harman thought he had won the election for London Mayor, BBC News, 2 May 2008

And as for Ken, Mayor Livingstone, I think you have been a very considerable public servant and a distinguished leader of this city. You shaped the office of mayor. You gave it national prominence and when London was attacked on 7 July 2005, you spoke for London. And I can tell you that with your courage and the sheer exuberant nerve with which you stuck it to your enemies, especially in New Labour, you have thereby earned the thanks and admiration of millions of Londoners, even if you think that they have a funny way of showing it today. And when we have that drink together which we both so richly deserve, I hope we can discover a way in which the mayoralty can continue to benefit from your transparent love of London, a city whose energy conquered the world and which now brings the world together in one city. I do not for one minute believe that this election shows that London has been transformed overnight into a Conservative city, but I do hope it does show that the Conservatives have changed into a party that can again be trusted after thirty years with the greatest, most cosmopolitan, multi-racial, generous-hearted city on earth, in which there are huge and growing divisions between rich and poor. And that brings me to my final thank-you, which is of course to the people of London. I would like to thank first the vast multitudes who voted against me – and I have met quite a few in the last nine months, not all of them entirely polite. I will work flat out from now on to earn your trust and to dispel some of the myths that have been created about me. And as for those who voted for me, I know there will be many whose pencils hovered for an instant before putting an X in my box and I will work flat out to repay and to justify your confidence. We have a new team ready to go into City Hall. Where there have been mistakes, we will rectify them. Where there are achievements, we will build on them. Where there are neglected opportunities, we will seize on them, and we will focus on the priorities of the people of London: cutting crime, improving transport, protecting green space, delivering affordable housing, giving taxpayers value for money in every one of the thirty-two boroughs. And I hope that everybody who loves this city will put aside party differences to try in the making of Greater London greater still. Let's get cracking tomorrow and let's have a drink tonight.

First speech as Mayor of London, City Hall, 3 May 2008

Boris Johnson: Whatever type of Wall's sausage is contrived by this great experiment, the dominant ingredient has got to be conservatism. The meat in the sausage has got to be Conservative, I would say. With plenty of bread and other bits and pieces.

Jeremy Paxman: The question is whether it's a chipolata or a Cumberland sausage, I suppose, is it?

BJ: This is fantastic to listen to. Enough of this gastronomic metaphor!

JP: You started it!

BJ: Well, I've had enough of it!

JP: Haven't you got a city to run?

BJ: I have got a city to run and that's exactly the point! The government of London will carry on irrespective of the temporary difficulties in providing a national government. Thank you.

JP: Bye, Boris!

On the possibility of a coalition after the UK general election, BBC News, 7 May 2010

Let me tell you, if they want a cut-price deal for a central London venue with a view of London landmarks, the ideal place would be City Hall.

Offering City Hall as a cheap venue for Prince William and Kate Middleton's wedding

It would be an utter travesty to blame these events on the police. The police did not riot. The police did not loot or recklessly set fire to property. The police did not attack innocent bystanders.

Evening Standard, **9 August 2011**

We can rebuild every part of the city that has been damaged; we can repair every shop; we can make sure that everyone understands the compensation to which they are entitled.

Boris staying resilient after the London riots

Just before I begin, can I check that we are all proud Conservatives – proud of the oldest and most successful party in all the Western democracies – and that we all intend to fight the next election under the Conservative banner? Am I right? Are there any quitters or splitters? Anyone feeling a bit yellow around the edges – like a kipper? The light is dawning. Scales falling. Across the country the chattering classes are waking up to the reality that victory is within our grasp in the next eight months. And we don't want to go back. Because I think things are going well, and on the verge of going even better. And I know there will be people who object that I am a mere municipal toenail; and that I am just the Mayor of that strange place called London where things are supposed to be so different. And to listen to some of the London-bashing you might think that London was a modern Babylon with billionaires being plied with hot towels in the top-deck club class of their swanky new buses. Or guzzling pearls dissolved in vinegar while lolling back on the padded cushions of their Barclays hire bikes. And if you pulled my toenails out I would confess that post-Olympic London is by most measures the most popular and successful city on earth.

Conservative Party conference, 30 September 2014

So, brick, my little friend, you will not be alone in London. That is a lot of work for the factories of the Midlands.

While holding a brick

They let me out of London sometimes, folks:

- to tie factories in Darwen where they are taking on more workers to satisfy the demand for cummerbunds, (in China, the cummerbund always having been an essential bit of Chinese communist apparel);
- to a shears factory in Gloucestershire that exports camel clippers to Mongolia – I am not making this up;
- a chili factory in Wiltshire that is making unbelievable million-Scoville chilis; and that is now working with the Indian government to supply weapons-strength chilis for crowd control – they'll be begging for water cannon after that stuff, believe me.

Conservative Party conference, 30 September 2014

Did you see George Clooney and Sandra Bullock in that wonderful film *Gravity*, cowering as the interstellar projectiles whanged past them like a couple of pensioners sheltering from Ed Miliband's new property taxes? Those asteroids didn't come from outer space; all of them manufactured in Soho.

Conservative Party conference, 30 September 2014

GETTING ELECTED

The dreadful truth is that when people come to see their MP, they have run out of better ideas.

Daily Telegraph, 18 September 2003

I will never vote to ban hunting. It is a piece of spite that has nothing to do with animal welfare, and everything to do with Blair's manipulation of rank-and-file Labour chippiness and class hatred.

Friends, Voters, Countrymen

It is impossible not to suffer a little frisson of fear about what may be beyond those hairy lips. You cannot help speculating about the slavering canine chops that may be right there, about to close over your intrusive politician's fingers.

On his fear of election leafleting

[The Building and Buildings, England and Wales regulation] is the 4,633rd regulation the government has introduced this year. If this government has any architectural legacy whatsoever, apart from the Dome, it will be a host of yawning unrepaired windows. It is through one of those apertures that they should chuck these and other regulations, before it is too late.

First-past-the-post has served this country well, and served dozens of other countries well. We would be mad to go to a great deal of trouble and expense to adopt a system that is less fair than the one we have.

On the Alternative Vote system

The whole point about representative democracy is not that it is perfectly representative of the views of the people, but that the representatives should do their duty by their consciences.

If Gordon Brown is on course to win the election, then Elvis Presley is on course to win *The X Factor* and Shergar to win the Grand National.

On Gordon Brown's chances of winning the forthcoming general election, 1 March 2010

I think Disraeli was once asked why people went to the House of Commons, and he said, 'We do it for fame.' And it was Achilles who said the thing is that fame or the desire to be known is not in itself necessarily disreputable. Achilles said he was doing it all for the glory of song and immortality.

Asked by Piers Morgan if he considered himself a celebrity

I don't know… Well, no, I'd like to be remembered as a politician.

Asked by Piers Morgan for which profession he would like to be remembered

It was meant to be the week when church bells were rung, coins struck, stamps issued and bonfires lit to send beacons of freedom from hilltop to hilltop. This was the Friday when Charles Moore's retainers were meant to be weaving through the moonlit lanes of Sussex, half blind with scrumpy, singing Brexit shanties at the tops of their voices and beating the hedgerows with staves. We are on the horns of a dilemma. We are between a rock and a hard place; the devil and the deep blue sea. We have on one side the Scylla of the backstop and on the other the Charybdis of infinite parliamentary delay. We have the frying pan labelled Theresa May and the fire consisting of the new triumvirate of Oliver Letwin, Yvette Cooper and Nick Boles.

On not leaving the EU on 29 March, *Daily Telegraph*, 26 March 2019

And so I am standing before you today, to tell you, the British people, that those critics are wrong – the doubters, the doomsters, the gloomsters are going to get it wrong again. The people who bet against Britain are going to lose their shirts because we are going to restore trust in our democracy. Never mind the backstop – the buck stops here.

Speech in Downing Street, 24 July 2019

LEFTIES, COMMIES AND OTHER DOOM-MONGERS

Labour's appalling agenda, encouraging the teaching of homosexuality in schools, and all the rest of it.

The Spectator, 15 April 2000

But here's old Ken – he's been crass, he's been insensitive and thuggish and brutal in his language – but I don't think actually, if you read what he said, although it was extraordinary and rude, I don't think he was actually antisemitic.

As snow-jobs go, this beats the Himalayas … It is just flipping unbelievable. He is a mixture of Harry Houdini and a greased piglet. He is barely human in his elusiveness. Nailing Blair is like trying to pin jelly to a wall.

Reaction to the Hutton Report, *Daily Telegraph*, 29 January 2004

I'd want to get Blair and really interrogate the guy. I'd really want to pin him up against a palm tree and slap him around and get the truth out of him about a few things. We need a bit of elucidation.

Ken [Livingstone] doesn't think he's got anything to say sorry for and if that's really his feeling, then I think that he should stick to his guns.

It's time they were ejected into outer space.
On the Labour Party, 2005

This is the government that promised to build a 'New Britain', that told us that 'things could only get better', and what was their salient commitment to the nation yesterday, apart from some hoary old bilge about drunken yobbery? It was to pick on a small group of a few thousand eccentrics who like to potter around the countryside on their horses, endlessly breaking their collarbones, and to tell them that whatever they're doing, they mustn't. This is government of the fox, for the fox, by the fox. Hunting is crucial to Labour, because it gives some contour to the semolina-like blob of Tony Blair's ideology. For the millions of Labour voters who have been depressed by the government's failures in the public services, it is one of the few overt chances they will get for class warfare; and conversely the quarrel over hunting enables Labour ministers to caricature their opponents as tweed-wearing Waugh-reading defenders of atavism.

Here we are in one of the most depressed downs in southern England, a place that is arguably too full of drugs, obesity, underachievement and Labour MPs.

GQ, 2007

In the Tuscan palazzo of Count Girolamo Strozzi … [Tony Blair] forged one of New Labour's few hard-edged ideological positions: he was pro-sciutto and anti-pasto.

Daily Telegraph, 22 July 2008

It is utterly absurd that Labour should be calling on us all to remember the value of that inclusive word 'British', when it is the government's own devolution programme which has fomented the rising sense of Scottishness and Englishness.

Lend Me Your Ears

You great big quivering gelatinous invertebrate jelly of indecision, you marched your troops up to the top of the hill in October of 2007. Show us that you've got enough guts to have an election 4 June. Gordon: Man or Mouse?!

Boris enticing Gordon Brown to call an election for June 2009,
Wall Street Journal, 3 January 2009

I will greatly miss Alan Johnson, not just because he is a nice guy but also for the satisfaction I used to get when I saw a headline saying, 'Johnson in new gaffe' and realised it wasn't me.

I was pleased to see that you called me a blond-haired mop in the papers. If I am a mop, David Cameron, you are a broom – a broom that is clearing up the mess left by the Labour government, and a fantastic job you are doing. I congratulate you and your colleagues George Osborne the dustpan, Michael Gove the jay-cloth, William Hague the sponge.

Addressing David Cameron at the Conservative Party conference, 9 October 2012

So let's leave Ed Balls to his football practice; and let's leave Ed Miliband to master the art of the bacon sarnie; and let's leave the Clegger to get on with whatever it is he does.

Conservative Party conference, 30 September 2014

I know this conference is going to be a staggering success because just in the last couple of days about a dozen far-left Momentum activists have kindly pledged their loyalty by ringing my private mobile phone. I put them straight on to Brandon [Lewis, party chair].

Conservative Party conference, 2 October 2018

We cannot, must not and will not let this weaselly cabal of superannuated Marxists and Hugo Chávez-admiring, antisemitism-condoning Kremlin apologists anywhere near the government of this country.

Conservative Party conference, 2 October 2018

I know their obsessions with strange far-left Latin American caudillos with proto-Marxist views and a curious hostility to free speech.

On the London Labour left, 12 June 2019

GREENERY

I am far too terrified to dissent from the growing world creed of global warming …

We need an alternative, and one that doesn't just involve crucifying our landscape with wind farms which, even when they are in motion, would barely pull the skin off a rice pudding.

Have I Got Views For You

We're not Hobbits. I am not about building homes for Hobbits.

On the average floor space in London homes, November 2008

There is something sacred about watching an elephant having breakfast in the wild.

Daily Telegraph, 7 October 2017

Sadiq Khan may be a twinkle-toed mover on the movie premiere red carpet, but his pirouettes on the subject of knife crime are a positive wonder.

Daily Telegraph, 22 July 2018

We are talking here not about some mildly satirical metaphors in a newspaper column; we are talking about a real plan – to take effect next summer – to begin again the brutal harpooning of beautiful, intelligent and endangered mammals. What is wrong with us all? Are we so bleared and crapulous with the effects of Christmas that we have somehow failed to take it in? Or perhaps, dear reader, I misjudge your own instincts. Perhaps you are unable to get too worked up about the fate of the whales. You may think that there are loads of them in the sea, and that turning them into whale sushi is a good way of using them up. Or maybe you have decided that we can't very well harp on about how intelligent whales are, when pigs are just as intelligent, if not even smarter, and we slaughter pigs by the million. Or it could be, I suppose, that you are instinctively sympathetic to whales, but there is something about all this eco-campaigning that sets your teeth on edge, and frankly there are times when you would like to see the last environmentalist strangled with the guts of the last rhino … Just you try being harpooned. You see how you like it.

On Japanese whaling, *Daily Telegraph*, 30 December 2018

Dear Extinction Rebellion: your aims are worthy, but take your pink boat to China instead … I am utterly fed up with being told by nice young people that their opinions are more important than my own – because they will be around a lot longer than me, and therefore that they have a greater stake in the future of the planet. With all due humility to my juniors, I intend to be alive for a very long time. Indeed, one of my few remaining ambitions is to be on the beach at Hastings to write a colour story, for the *Telegraph*, on the thousandth anniversary of the Norman landings in 2066. My map tells me that London is nearer to Beijing than it is to Los Angeles. Surely this is the time for the protesters to take their pink boat to Tiananmen Square, and lecture them in the way they have been lecturing us. Whether the Chinese will allow them to block the traffic is another matter.

On Extinction Rebellion, 21 April 2019

If you are an incorrigible old Lefty like Jeremy Corbyn, you see the problem of global warming as the perfect excuse for government to tax, ban, nanny, finger-wag and generally bully anyone involved in any kind of economic activity – especially business. Let Corbyn and Co knit their own hempen vests and make their own toothpaste.

Daily Telegraph, 9 June 2019

BREXIT AND OTHER STORIES

I am not by any means an ultra-Eurosceptic. In some ways, I am a bit of a fan of the European Union. If we did not have one, we would invent something like it.

House of Commons, 2003

If Amsterdam or Leningrad vie for the title of Venice of the North, then Venice – what compliment is high enough? Venice, with all her civilisation and ancient beauty, Venice with her addiction to curious aquatic means of transport, yes, my friends, Venice is the Henley of the South.

Daily Telegraph, 11 March 2004

It is a wonder that the Dutch look so tall and healthy, when you consider what they eat.

Lend Me Your Ears

All those snooty Europhile politicians and journalists who sneered at us for our doubts should be forced to crawl in penitence to Dublin Castle, scourging themselves with copies of the Maastricht Treaty. We have been vindicated, and the least they can do is admit it.

Daily Telegraph, 13 December 2010

By all means let us have a referendum – the one we were promised, on the Lisbon EU Treaty.

28 February 2011

We will remain a paid-up ... valued participating member of the single market. Under no circumstances in my view will a British government ... adjust that position.

Speaking at an IPPR/Centre for London event, and reported on *Channel 4 News,* 2011

So we can only wonder what madness took hold at the judging lunch the other day, when that committee of Norwegian worthies was asked to appoint this year's winner of the prize. Perhaps they were drunk; perhaps it was one of those morose Scandinavian afternoons when the sun has sunk and there is no alternative but to hit the aquavit. Whatever it was, they must have been out of their minds to ignore all human candidates and award the prize to the European Union. And for bringing peace to Europe! You might as well offer recognition to Lance Armstrong for his role in promoting good sportsmanship. You might as well suggest that Sir Jimmy Savile deserves some other posthumous gong for his egregious 'charity' work.

On the EU winning the Nobel Peace Prize, *Daily Telegraph*, **15 October 2012**

Don't forget that fifteen years ago the entire CBI, British industry, the City, everybody was prophesying that there would be gigantic mutant rats with gooseberry eyes swarming out of the gutters in the sewer to gnaw the last emaciated faces of the remaining British bankers because we didn't go into the euro.

The Andrew Marr Show, **16 December 2012**

We can no longer blame Brussels. This is perhaps the most important point of all. If we left the EU, we would end this sterile debate, and we would have to recognise that most of our problems are not caused by 'Bwussels', but by chronic British short-termism, inadequate management, sloth, low skills, a culture of easy gratification and under-investment in both human and physical capital and infrastructure.

Daily Telegraph, 12 May 2013

We welcome all sorts of luminaries to City Hall, but not so long ago I welcomed the former French Prime Minister, Monsieur Alain Juppé, to my office in City Hall and he cruised in with his sizeable retinue of very distinguished fellows with their Légion d'honneur floret and all the rest of it and we shook hands and had a tête-a-tête and he told me that he was now the Mayor of Bordeaux. I think he may have been Mayor of Bordeaux when he was Prime Minister, it's the kind of thing they do in France – a very good idea in my view. Joke, joke, joke! And what he said … joke! He said that he had the honour of representing, he had 239,517 people in Bordeaux and therefore he had the honour of representing the ninth biggest city in France. I got the ball back very firmly over the net, folks, because I said there were 250,000 French men and women in London and therefore I was the mayor of the sixth biggest French city on earth.

On former French Prime Minister and Mayor of Bordeaux Alain Juppé at the Conservative Party conference, as reported in *The Spectator*, 5 October 2013

The EU would be a lobster … because the EU, by the very way it works, encourages its participating members to order the lobster at the joint meal because they know that the bill is going to be settled by everybody else – normally by the Germans.

When asked if the EU were an animal, what animal would it be?
Daily Telegraph, 12 May 2014

We are seeing a slow and invisible process of legal colonisation, as the EU infiltrates just about every area of public policy.

Sometimes these EU rules sound simply ludicrous, like the rule that you can't recycle a teabag, or that children under eight cannot blow up balloons, or the limits on the power of vacuum cleaners.

I'm rather pro-European, actually. I certainly want a European community where one can go and scoff croissants, drink delicious coffee, learn foreign languages and generally make love to foreign women.

Daily Telegraph, February 2016

You look at the plan to increase the efforts to prop up the single currency with an ever denser system of integration, with more and more regulation about all sorts of social and economic issues which will impact directly on this country, I think the risk is increasingly in staying in the project. I think the best thing we can do is show a lead, show an example and strike out for freedom.

BBC News, 11 March 2016

I can read novels in French and I can sing the 'Ode to Joy' in German, and if they keep accusing me of being a Little Englander, I will. Both as editor of *The Spectator* and Mayor of London I have promoted the teaching of modern European languages in our schools. I have dedicated much of my life to the study of the origins of our common European culture and civilisation in ancient Greece and Rome. So I find it offensive, insulting, irrelevant and positively cretinous to be told – sometimes by people who can barely speak a foreign language – that I belong to a group of small-minded xenophobes.

ConservativeHome, 9 May 2016

Napoleon, Hitler, various people tried this out, and it ends tragically. The EU is an attempt to do this by different methods.

Arguing that the European Union aims to create a powerful superstate, *Daily Telegraph*, **14 May 2016**

If you want to back the entrepreneurs, the grafters, the workers, the innovators, the burgeoning and dynamic businesses of Britain – then Vote Leave on 23 June, and give this cabal the kick in the pants they deserve.

Daily Telegraph, **15 May 2016**

It's 24 June and quite early in the morning – too early, frankly. You wake up with a vague but intensifying sense of guilt, and wonder why you have fallen asleep on the sofa. There are half-drunk beer cans lying around, crisp packets. The TV is burbling to itself in the corner of the room, and you know that in a second you are going to remember that something big has happened, and that you aren't going to like it – and then it hits you: the Referendum! That's right.

Daily Telegraph, **5 June 2016**

Take back control of huge sums of money, £350 million a week, and spend it on our priorities such as the NHS.
9 June 2016

I have known David Cameron for a very long time, and I believe he has been one of the most extraordinary politicians of our age. A brave and principled man, who has given superb leadership of his party and his country for many years … I think that the electorate have searched in their hearts and answered as best they can in a poll the scale the like of which we have never seen before in this country. They have decided it is time to vote to take back control from an EU that has become too opaque and not accountable enough to the people it is meant to serve … But there is simply no need in the twenty-first century to be part of a federal government in Brussels that is imitated nowhere else on Earth. It was a noble idea for its time but it is no longer right for this country.
Speech at Vote Leave HQ, 24 June 2016

What exactly is it about the EU that attracts the fervent admiration of north London radicals? It was the first time I had ever heard of trendy socialists demonstrating in favour of an unelected supranational bureaucracy.

On people protesting outside his house, 3 July 2016

There is no plan for no deal, because we're going to get a great deal.

PoliticsHome, 11 July 2017

Philip Hollobone: Since we joined the common market on 1 January 1973 until the day we leave, we will have given the EU and its predecessors, in today's money, in real terms, a total of £209 billion. Will you make it clear to the EU that if they want a penny piece more then they can go whistle?

Boris Johnson: I'm sure that my hon. Friend's words will have broken like a thunderclap over Brussels and they will pay attention to what he has said. He makes a very valid point and I think that the sums that I have seen that they propose to demand from this country seem to me to be extortionate and I think 'to go whistle' is an entirely appropriate expression.

At the dispatch box in the House of Commons after Philip Hollobone, a Eurosceptic Tory MP, pressed him to reject requests for a multi-billion-pound exit payment,
The Guardian, 11 July 2017

The trouble is that I have practised the words over the weekend and find that they stick in the throat.

On his resignation as Foreign Secretary over May's Brexit deal, *The Guardian,* **9 July 2018**

We have wrapped a suicide vest around the British constitution – and handed the detonator to [EU chief negotiator] Michel Barnier.

On Theresa May's Brexit strategy, *The Guardian,* **9 September 2018**

I hesitated, as you hesitate these days on meeting someone with strong but unknown views on Brexit. Will they slobber on your cheeks or try to take your head off?

On meeting Saba the cheetah, *Daily Telegraph,* **17 February 2019**

Theresa May is a chicken who's bottled Brexit.
Daily Telegraph, 24 March 2019

We need to realise the depth of the problems we face. Unless we get on and do this thing, we will be punished for a very long time. There is a very real choice between getting Brexit done and the potential extinction of this great party.
BBC News, 5 June 2019

It is absolutely vital that we prepare for a no-deal Brexit if we are going to get a deal. But I don't think that is where we are going to end up – I think it is a million-to-one against – but it is vital that we prepare.
Conservative leadership hustings, 26 June 2019

If you want to understand why it is that we must leave the EU and the advantages of coming out, I want you to consider this kipper which has been presented to me just now by the editor of a national newspaper who received it from a kipper smoker in the Isle of Man who is utterly furious because after decades of sending kippers like this through the post, he has had his costs massively increased by Brussels bureaucrats who insist that each kipper must be accompanied by this, a plastic ice pillow. Pointless, expensive, environmentally-damaging health and safety, ladies and gentlemen. When we come out, therefore, we will not only be able to end this damaging regulatory overkill, but we will also be able to do things to boost Britain's economy and we will be able to establish an identity as a truly global Britain and get our mojo back.

Evening Standard, 17 July 2019

I prophesy very confidently that we will have a successful Brexit, the planes will fly, there will be clean drinking water and there will be whey for the Mars bars. Because where there's a will there's a whey.

The Scotsman, 17 July 2019

First they make us pay in our taxes for Greek olive groves, many of which probably don't exist. Then they say we can't dip our bread in olive oil in restaurants. We didn't join the Common Market – betraying the New Zealanders and their butter – in order to be told when, where and how we must eat the olive oil we have been forced to subsidise. Talk about giving us the pip, folks.

The Scotsman, 17 July 2019

We are volunteering for economic vassalage, not just in goods and agrifoods, but we will be forced to match EU arrangements on the environment and social affairs and much else besides…

The problem is not that we failed to make the case for a Free Trade Agreement of the kind spelt out at Lancaster House. We haven't even tried. We must try now, because we will not have another chance to get this right. It is absolute nonsense to imagine – as I fear some of my colleagues do – that we can somehow afford to make a botched Treaty now, and then break and reset the bone later on. We have seen even in these talks how the supposedly provisional becomes eternal.

ConservativeHome, 18 July 2019

They went to the Moon fifty years ago. Surely today we can solve the logistical issues of the Irish border.

Daily Telegraph, 21 July 2019

TORIES, SACKINGS AND RESIGNATIONS

Among the many reasons for mourning the passing of Auberon Waugh is that he will not be here to witness the final obliteration of hunting by the Labour Party … If I were not a Tory, I think I would become one on this issue alone.

Daily Telegraph, 18 January 2001

Look the point is … Er, what is the point? It is a tough job but somebody has got to do it.

On being appointed shadow Arts Minister, 7 May 2004

My friends, as I have discovered myself, there are no disasters, only opportunities. And, indeed, opportunities for fresh disasters.

On being sacked from the Tory front bench, *Daily Telegraph*, 2 December 2004

Tremendous, little short of superb. On cracking form.

Asked how he was feeling after being sacked as shadow Arts Minister for having misled Michael Howard

Nothing excites compassion, in friend and foe alike, as much as the sight of you ker-splonked on the tarmac with your propeller buried six feet under.

On being sacked from the Tory front bench, *Daily Telegraph*, 2 December 2004

I'm making absolutely no comment … And no, I did not.

When asked if he intentionally misled Michael Howard, leader of the Conservative Party

Give that man a handbag! And while you're at it, tell him to wear a powder blue suit and a pineapple coloured wig next time he wants to impersonate this century's greatest peacetime Prime Minister.

Lend Me Your Ears

Mrs Thatcher pioneered a revolution that was imitated, in one way or another, around the world.

Lend Me Your Ears

I'm having Sunday lunch with my family. I'm vigorously campaigning, inculcating my children in the benefits of a Tory government.

The Guardian, 11 April 2005

Howard is a dynamic performer on many levels. There you are. He sent me to Liverpool. Marvellous place. Howard was the most effective Home Secretary since Peel. Hang on, was Peel Home Secretary?

On Michael Howard, *The Times*, 19 April 2005

We will demonstrate that we are the party that cares about the older generation by propelling a man who is so full of vim he will give me a thrashing on the squash court and has nine-and-a-half grandchildren.

Trying to get his dad elected in Teignbridge, 2005

Celebrating. I do think there's every chance. There's a swing on.

When asked what he will be doing the day after the election, 2005

We can be as nice as pie, we can take our ties off and breakdance down the esplanade and all wear earrings and all the rest of it. It won't make any difference to the electorate if they don't think we're going to offer a new and improved, basically Conservative approach to government.

Conservative Party conference, 2005

I think they get a fair squeeze of the sauce bottle.

Questioned by Michael Crick on his dedication to his political career and the Conservative Party, 2005

I have successfully ridden two horses for quite a long time. But I have to admit there have been moments when the distance between the two horses has grown terrifyingly wide, and I did momentarily come off.

Reflecting on his very public 2004 downfall, November 2005

It may be that the psychological effort needed to haul myself around into a more gaffe-free zone proves too difficult.

When asked if he was due to be included in the latest Tory reshuffle, June 2007

Statistically, I am due to be fired again.

When asked if he was due to be included in the latest Tory reshuffle, June 2007

If we Tories wished to reverse just one year's growth in Whitehall, we would have to sack the equivalent of the entire population of Ilfracombe, the seaside town in Devon!

Piers Morgan: Do you expect a Cabinet post if Cameron wins?

Boris Johnson: I don't know … My grandmother always said, 'It's not how you're doing, it's what you're doing.' And I think it will get easier when there is a big job to do and I can get on and do it. These points you make about image and buffoonery will fall away.

WHEN THE BALL
IS RELEASED FROM
THE SCRUM

There is no need here to rehearse the steps of matricide. Howe pounced, Heseltine did his stuff. After it was all over, my wife, Marina, claimed she came upon me, stumbling down a street in Brussels, tears in my eyes, and claiming that it was as if someone had shot Nanny.

On the fall of Margaret Thatcher, *Lend Me Your Ears*

I have as much chance of becoming Prime Minister as of being decapitated by a frisbee or of finding Elvis.

Daily Mail, 22 July 2003

I'm backing David Cameron's campaign out of pure, cynical self-interest.

On the 2005 Conservative leadership contest, *The Independent*, 5 October 2005

I haven't got a cat's chance in hell of becoming Prime Minister … But as I've said before, if I was called from my plough to serve in head office, then obviously I would do my best.

On his future career

My chances of being PM are about as good as the chances of finding Elvis on Mars, or my being reincarnated as an olive.

Will I throw my hat into the ring? It depends on what kind of ring it is and what kind of hat I have in my hand.

When asked by the *Oxford Mail* if he would stand for leader of the Conservative Party

Hello, I'm your MP. Actually, I'm not. I'm your candidate. Gosh.

Canvassing in Henley, 2005

All politicians in the end are like crazed wasps in a jam jar, each individually convinced that they are going to make it.

On his political ambitions, November 2005

My ambition silicon chip has been programmed to try to scramble up this ladder, so I do feel a kind of sense that I have got to.

Describing his political ambitions, November 2005

It is vital now to see this [Brexit] moment for what it is. This is not a time to quail, it is not a crisis, nor should we see it as an excuse for wobbling or self-doubt, but it is a moment for hope and ambition for Britain. A time not to fight against the tide of history, but to take that tide at the flood, and sail on to fortune.

During the announcement that he would not run to become Britain's Prime Minister, 30 June 2016. A reference to Brutus's 'There is a tide in the affairs of men. Which, taken at the flood, leads on to fortune' in *Julius Caesar*

Now, I'm no Communist. As my time in City Hall will testify, I'm a tax-cutting Conservative ... And I'm proud to say that at the end of eight years not only is everyone living longer, eighteen months longer both for men and for women, as I tell you, you live longer under the Conservatives. The biggest gains in life expectancy have been made by those with the lowest incomes ... I will not pretend that everything has always been rosy; things are sometimes tough, even in the greatest city on Earth. I've led the capital through riots and blizzards and strikes and terrorist attack, and every time we have bounced back and gone from strength to strength ... Well, I ask you to look at our capital today, still the number one financial centre, the greatest tech hub in this hemisphere, the number one tourist destination on Earth, with more visitors going to the British Museum, I'm told, than go to the whole of Belgium, not that I have anything against Brussels at all, as you know.

Announcement that he would not be entering the Conservative leadership race, 30 June 2016

On rumours that he would quit after May's Brexit speech: Not me, guv. I don't know where it is coming from, honestly. It feels to me like an attempt to keep the great snore-athon story about my article running. I think that is what is going on.

The Guardian, 19 September 2017

I thought it was the right vision then. I think so today.

But in the eighteen months that have followed, it is as though a fog of self-doubt has descended. Even though our EU friends and partners liked the Lancaster House vision – it was what they were expecting from an ambitious partner, and what they understood – even though the commentators liked it, and the markets liked it (the pound soared), we never actually went to Brussels and turned it into a negotiating offer.

Instead we dithered. We burned through negotiating capital. We agreed to hand over a £40 billion exit fee, with no discussion of our future economic relationship. We accepted the jurisdiction of the European Court over key aspects of the withdrawal agreement. And, worst of all, we allowed the question of the Northern Irish border, which had hitherto been assumed on all sides to be readily soluble, to become so politically charged as to dominate the debate.

No one wants a hard border. You couldn't construct one if you tried. But there certainly can be different rules north and south of the border to reflect the fact that there are two different jurisdictions. In fact, there already are.

There can be checks away from the border, and technical solutions, as the PM described at Mansion House, and in fact, there already are.

Resignation statement, House of Commons, 18 July 2018

I believe I am best placed to lift this party, beat Jeremy Corbyn and excite people about conservatism and conservative values.

BBC News, 5 June 2019

Hannah Vaughan Jones: Can you give an example, in your political life, when you've set your own self-interest aside for the benefit of the country?

Boris Johnson: Well, er, pfft, um, it's a good question, but er, I, I, I would, you know, I don't, obviously, it's an embarrassing but, but true that, um, er, it is obviously, possible, er, how should I put this, to make more money, er, by not being a full-time politician. Um, I don't, I don't want to put too fine a point on it, er, but, you know, you have to, you have to, you have to, make sacrifices sometimes.

Conservative leadership contest hustings in Darlington, 5 July 2019

PRIME MINISTER

I have just been to see Her Majesty the Queen, who has invited me to form a government and I have accepted. I pay tribute to the fortitude and patience of my predecessor and her deep sense of public service, but in spite of all her efforts it has become clear that there are pessimists at home and abroad who think that after three years of indecision that this country has become a prisoner to the old arguments of 2016 and that in this home of democracy we are incapable of honouring a basic democratic mandate ... The people who bet against Britain are going to lose their shirts because we are going to restore trust in our democracy and we are going to fulfil the repeated promises of Parliament to the people and come out of the EU on 31 October, no ifs or buts, and we will do a new deal, a better deal that will maximise the opportunities of Brexit while allowing us to develop a new and exciting partnership with the rest of Europe based on free trade and mutual support ... Everyone knows the values that flag represents. It stands for freedom and free speech and habeas corpus and the rule of law, and above all it stands for democracy and that is why we will come out of the EU on 31 October because in the end Brexit was a fundamental decision by the British people that they wanted their laws made by people that they can elect and they can remove from office and we must now respect that decision and create a new partnership with our European friends – as warm and as close and as affectionate as possible and the first step is to repeat unequivocally our guarantee to the 3.2 million EU nationals now living and working among us, and I say directly to you – thank you for your contribution to our society, thank you for your patience and I can assure you that under this government you will get the absolute certainty of the rights to live and remain … No one in the last few centuries has succeeded in betting against the pluck and nerve and ambition of this country. They will not succeed today. We in this government will work flat out to give this country the leadership it deserves, and that work begins now.

First speech as Prime Minister, 24 July 2019

Mr Speaker, I, with permission, shall make a statement on the mission of this new Conservative government … Over these past few years, too many people in this country feel that they have been told repeatedly and relentlessly what we cannot do.

Since I was a child I remember respectable authorities asserting that our time as a nation has passed, that we should be content with mediocrity and managed decline …

And time and again, by their powers to innovate and adapt, the British people have showed the doubters wrong.

And, Mr Speaker, I believe that at this pivotal moment in our national story we are going to prove the doubters wrong again.

Not just with positive thinking and a can-do attitude, important though they are.

But with the help and the encouragement of a government and a Cabinet who are bursting with ideas, ready to create change and determined to implement the policies we need to succeed as a nation.

The greatest place to live.

The greatest place to bring up a family.

The greatest place to send your kids to school.

The greatest place to set up a business or to invest.

Because we have the best transport and the cleanest environment and the best healthcare and the most compassionate approach to care of elderly people.

That is the mission of the Cabinet I have appointed.

That is the purpose of the government I am leading.

And that is why I believe that if we bend our sinews

to the task now, there is every chance that in 2050, when I fully intend to be around, although not necessarily in this job we will look back on this period, this extraordinary period, as the beginning of a new golden age for our United Kingdom.

And I commend this future to the House just as much as I commend this statement.

Statement to the House of Commons, 25 July 2019

OTHERS ON BORIS

A wise guy playing the fool to win.

Sunday Times, 16 July 2000

You are a self-centred, pompous twit. Even your body language on TV is pathetic. Get out of public life. Go and do something in the private sector.

Paul Bigley, brother of murdered hostage Kenneth Bigley,
to Johnson on Radio City in Liverpool, 21 October 2004

People always ask me the same question, they say, 'Is Boris a very clever man pretending to be an idiot?' And I always say, 'No.'

Ian Hislop on *Parkinson*, 19 November 2006

For all his taste for comedy, he has done nothing as inherently comic as Mayor Livingstone's risible cultivation of the Venezuelan President, Hugo Chávez. It should be asked: who is the real 'joke candidate' here?

The Spectator, 21 July 2007

He may seem like a lovable buffoon but you know he wouldn't hesitate to line you all up against a wall and have you shot.

Jeremy Hardy on Radio 4

What the f*** are you doing here?

A drug dealer, as Boris burst into the man's house as part of a police raid

He's the sort of person who 200 years ago would have died aged thirty leading a cavalry charge into a volcano.

Frankie Boyle on *Mock the Week*

A bicycle permanently chained to the railings of Downing Street. A blond head bobbing up and down at *Prime Minister's Questions*. Visiting world leaders receiving lectures in Latin. If David Cameron, George Osborne and their coalition fail, one leading Conservative can say that his hands were clean. Untouched by the compromises of coalition, Boris Johnson is styling himself as the true Conservative.

Tim Montgomerie imagines life under Prime Minister Boris

The Mayor of London is clearly the only senior politician with an ounce of sense.

Nigel Farage

You can never say it enough times, the Mayor of London Boris Johnson is a weird guy.

Le Monde, **2012**

Boris is a Chaucerian figure. Cameron is very keen on marriage – you would never catch Boris preaching about that. If Cameron was caught in bed with some bird, that would probably be the end of him, whereas Boris is so often pretty much caught in bed with some bird – but, you know, people rather expect that.

Andrew Gimson, Boris's biographer, *Newsweek*, April 2012

If Boris ever becomes PM, I'm on the first plane out of Britain … He is an authentic star, who lights up every room he enters. He makes people laugh and feel good. He sings a song that the British people – who despise almost every other politician in the pack – will crowd any venue to hear. Why should he not be Prime Minister? Why should Boris not be the man to leap forward and save the Conservative Party and the country from the dark forces? My own answer is that if the Mayor of London is the answer, there is something desperately wrong with the question … Most politicians are ambitious and ruthless, but Boris is a gold medal egomaniac.

Max Hastings, *Daily Mail*, 9 October 2012

You're a nasty piece of work, aren't you?

Eddie Mair, BBC One, March 2013

A canny player of the political game.

Michael Cockerell, March 2013

Most politicians, as far as I can work out, are pretty incompetent, and then have a veneer of competence, you do seem to do it the other way around.

Jeremy Clarkson, *Top Gear*

There's no point trying to contain Boris. He's mayor of London, he can speak out if he wants to.

David Cameron, *Daily Telegraph*, 6 October 2012

[The Conservatives] must concentrate on the fact they're dealing with a fairly lazy tosser who just wants to be there.

Ken Livingstone, *The Spectator*, 30 April 2014

I'm a big fan of his ... I think he's terrific, from an environmental point of view he is terrific, he's a great conservative, he's a great leader, he's interested in making business grow and he has a great personality. I remember he took me to the Olympics, made me watch the basketball, the finals and all this stuff. Going basically riding with him. They made the Boris bikes. Imagine what kind of great leadership that is. He started the Boris bikes, and they have them in France and they have them in Berlin, and then in Austria, all over. In America, in New York they have the bikes. Everyone copied London ... That just shows you what kind of a leader you have.

Arnold Schwarzenegger, LBC, May 2014

Don't be blinded by the relentless showmanship and the buffoonish charms of 'Boris' the brand … This 'Boris' is a hard target to hurt. Hitting him is not so difficult. Doing him damage is a much tougher task. Even when he seems to have done harm to himself, he sustains no obvious wounds. If anything, he grows stronger.

Dave Hill, *The Spectator*, 13 January 2015

I am surprised and disappointed that you have chosen to repeat the figure of £350 million per week, in connection with the amount that might be available for extra public spending when we leave the European Union. This confuses gross and net contributions. It also assumes that payments currently made to the UK by the EU, including for example for the support of agriculture and scientific research, will not be paid by the UK government when we leave. It is a clear misuse of official statistics.

Open letter to Boris Johnson from David Norgrove, chair of the UK Statistics Authority, 17 September 2017

Boris is a curious guy … There are no Johnsonites.

Nick Boles MP, 13 June 2019

I have known Johnson since the 1980s, when I edited the *Daily Telegraph* and he was our flamboyant Brussels correspondent. I have argued for a decade that, while he is a brilliant entertainer who made a popular maître d' for London as its mayor, he is unfit for national office, because it seems he cares for no interest save his own fame and gratification ... Yet the Tories have elevated a cavorting charlatan to the steps of Downing Street, and they should expect to pay a full forfeit when voters get the message ... If the price of Johnson proves to be Corbyn, blame will rest with the Conservative party, which is about to foist a tasteless joke upon the British people – who will not find it funny for long.

Max Hastings, *Daily Mirror*, 26 June 2019

I really admire Boris's ability to answer the question. I think he has this great ability – you ask him a question, he puts a smile on your face, and you forget what the question was. It's a brilliant quality for a politician, maybe not a Prime Minister though.

Jeremy Hunt MP, ITV debate, 9 July 2019

He's a fully paid-up member of the Donald Trump fan club.

Sir Nigel Sheinwald, diplomat, *Business Insider*, 11 July 2019

When I arrived in the Mayor's private office I still remember 'Welcome, welcome, welcome. Sit there. It's the only part of the building that's secure. Everywhere else, leftists everywhere. And whatever you do, don't go to the fifth floor without a guard, preferably armed.'

Guto Harri, *The Times*, 21 July 2019

We have a really good man is going to be the Prime Minister of the UK now. Boris Johnson. Good man, he's tough and he's smart. They're saying Britain Trump. They call him Britain Trump. And people are saying that's a good thing. They like me over there. That's what they wanted. That's what they need. It's what they need. He'll get it done, Boris is good, he's going to do a good job.

President Trump, 23 July 2019

[A] pound-shop Churchill impressionist.

Layla Moran MP

I don't know why anyone would want the job.

HM The Queen to Boris Johnson, 24 July 2019

I don't share his optimism about his opinion of himself … He's a charlatan. That is the clear evidence of his career and the way he has operated politically … Those of us who have worked alongside him and had a chance of watching him can see for ourselves his modus operandi and his capacity both for deception and self-deception and those are the two ingredients of charlatanism.

Dominic Grieve, Sky News, 24 July 2019

Boris is a weak man posing as a tough guy.

Nick Cohen, *The Spectator*, 24 July 2019

Q&A WITH BORIS

THE INDEPENDENT,
2 JANUARY 2007

How can somebody as fat as you get so many good-looking women to find you attractive?

Ardal Conyngham, Belfast

This strikes me as a trap question.

Have you ever taken illegal drugs? If not, why not?

Lois Beene, Cardiff

I have and I want you to know that I inhaled. Then I sneezed.

Do you ever harbour lustful thoughts about the honourable women members sitting opposite you on the House of Commons benches? If yes, which ones?

Steve Cant, Hastings

They are all perfectly lovely in their own ways. I am rather shocked that you should ask.

The people of Liverpool are a crowd of mawkish whingers. Why did you apologise?

Jim Bernard, Manchester

In the course of my inglorious pilgrimage of penitence I tried to distinguish between *The Spectator*'s attack on a general culture of sentimentality and grievance – which I stood by – and some offensive errors of fact about Hillsborough, for which I grovelled.

You confessed to having had a crush on Polly Toynbee. What is it about Polly that seems to drive Tory boys wild?
Tom Scarsdale, by email
Oh Lord. It's just she's so bossy and posh. Is that the right answer?

Have the Ancient Romans anything to teach the Tories about power?
Gabriella Kruse, Bristol
Yeah – that it's easily lost to the Vandals.

Who is your historical pin-up, and why?
Amelia Lancaster, Derby
Pericles. Look at his funeral speech. Democracy. Freedom. Champion stuff.

Are education standards slipping in Britain?

Richard Morris, Luton

Slipping! How could you even suggest it? Every year, comrades, our children are getting better and better at passing exams! Every year we produce more A*–C grade tractors from the Red Star plant! This year an amazing 43.5 per cent of candidates got an A at maths A-level, and guess what the proportion was forty years ago, when far fewer people took maths A-level? It was only 7 per cent! Now you do the maths. Oh, all right, I'll do it for you. That is a staggering 620 per cent improvement by our young geniuses. Let me enter the usual political guff about how hard everyone has worked, and let me congratulate them on their grades. But if too many CVs read like a man falling off a build-ing then the A is useless as a tool of differentiation, and that is why some universities are calling for a pre-U exam to replace A-levels, and that is why there is in-creasing interest in the IB. We have all connived in the fiction that our kids are getting brighter, because that conceals the growing gulf in attainment between much of the maintained sector and the grammar schools/ independent schools. The result is that the market has, inevitably, asserted itself, and in a way that is socially regressive. Which schools, after all, are going to have the resources to prepare their pupils for these new specialised university entrance exams?

QUICK FIRE
WITH IAIN DALE

Mayor of London or Prime Minister?
Mayor of London! Since it's the best job in the world.

Guilty pleasure?
Painting cheese boxes.

Thing you most hate about yourself?
Hotly contested field… [long pause] I suppose I'd love to lose a stone and a half.

Thing you love about yourself?
Oh Christ, that really is a hotly disputed area. I don't know. I have a very happy life. I find I'm capable of enjoying almost everything.

Favourite view?
I had the most amazing view of London as I came in from Davos. We circled over the whole city. It's just unbelievable. I realised how utility imposes a pattern on development and how common sense increments to the city produce this absolutely beautiful mosaic of life.

The book you are reading at the moment?
I'm reading about fifteen books at the moment. I've just read *Exile* by Denise Mina. The climax is not for the faint-hearted. It will leave you breathless and stunned.

Favourite film?
Dodgeball or *The Godfather.*

Political hero?
Pericles of Athens.

Political villain?
Alcibiades [Ancient Greek politician, famous for his role in the later stages of the Peloponnesian War].

Part of your body you love the most?
My leg you keep pulling.

THE BORIS BIBLIOGRAPHY

BY BORIS JOHNSON

Friends, Voters, Countrymen (HarperCollins, 2001)
Lend Me Your Ears (HarperCollins, 2003)
Seventy-Two Virgins (HarperCollins, 2004)
The Dream of Rome (HarperCollins, 2006)
Have I Got Views For You (HarperCollins, 2006)
Aspire Ever Higher (Politeia, 2006)
Life in the Fast Lane (HarperCollins, 2007)
Perils of the Pushy Parents (HarperCollins, 2007)
The British (HarperCollins, 2011)
Johnson's Life of London (HarperCollins, 2012)
The Churchill Factor (Hodder & Stoughton, 2015)

BY OTHERS

Boris: The Rise of Boris Johnson, Andrew Gimson (Simon & Schuster, 2007)
Boris v. Ken: How Boris Johnson Won London, Giles Edwards and Jonathan Isaby (Politico's Publishing, 2008)
Just Boris, Sonia Purnell (Aurum Press, 2012)

ABOUT THE AUTHORS

IAIN DALE presents the evening show on LBC and hosts the *For the Many* and *Iain Dale All Talk* podcasts. He is one of Britain's leading political commentators, appearing regularly on *Newsnight*, *The Andrew Marr Show* and *Good Morning Britain*. He is a visiting professor of politics and broadcasting at the University of East Anglia.

JAKUB SZWEDA is a graduate in media and communication and is a radio producer, currently working at LBC Radio.